The PreHistory of THE FAR SIDE
A 10th Anniversary Exhibit

by Gary Larson

KT-415-254

Other Books in The Far Side Series

The Far Side
Beyond The Far Side
In Search of The Far Side
Bride of The Far Side
Valley of The Far Side
It Came From The Far Side
Hound of The Far Side
The Far Side Observer
Night of the Crash-Test Dummies
Wildlife Preserves
Wiener Dog Art
Unnatural Selections
Cows of our Planet

Anthologies
The Far Side Gallery
The Far Side Gallery 2
The Far Side Gallery 3

The PreHistory of
THE FAR SIDE
A 10th Anniversary Exhibit

by Gary Larson

WARNER BOOKS

A *Warner* Book

First published in Great Britain in 1990
by Macdonald & Co (Publishers) Ltd

An edition published in 1991 by Futura Publications
Reprinted 1991 (twice)
This edition published in 1992 by Warner Books
Reprinted 1992

Copyright © 1980, 1981, 1982, 1984 by the
Chronicle Publishing Company
Copyright © 1984, 1985, 1986, 1987, 1988, 1989 by
Universal Press Syndicate

Cartoons on pages 26 and 27 copyright © 1976 by
Pacific Northwest Magazine. Reprinted by permission.
Cartoons on pages 28–33 copyright © 1979 *Seattle Times*.
Reprinted by permission.

All rights reserved.
No part of this publication may be reproduced,
stored in a retrieval system, or transmitted, in any
form or by any means, without the prior
permission in writing of the publisher, nor be
otherwise circulated in any form of binding or
cover other than that in which it is published and
without a similar condition including this
condition being imposed on the subsequent purchaser.

ISBN 0 7515 0419 X

Printed and bound in Great Britain by
BPCC Hazells Ltd
Member of BPCC Ltd

Warner Books
A Division of
Little, Brown and Company (UK) Limited
165 Great Dover Street
London SE1 4YA

*Tragedy is when I cut my finger.
Comedy is when you walk into an
open sewer and die.*
—MEL BROOKS

Contents

FOREWORD

On this, the tenth anniversary of drawing The Far Side, I thought it might be time to reveal some of the background, anecdotes, foibles, and "behind-the-scenes" experiences related to this cartoon panel. (This may or may not be of particular interest to anyone, but my therapist says it should do *me* a lot of good.)

What the reader will find herein is a chronicle of The Far Side's birth and evolution, complete with examples of various mutations (i.e., confusing or controversial cartoons) and annotations along the way of comments from either readers or myself. Via my sketchbooks, I've also included a glimpse (you wouldn't want to look closer) into the way my mind works in coming up with and developing cartoon ideas.

Finally, this book contains an "exhibit" of my personal favorite cartoons from The Far Side series since its inception on January 1, 1980. Keeping in that vein, I've not intended this section to be so much a "walk down memory lane" as I have an assemblage of The Far Side cartoons that I feel best reflect something of my own perspective on humor and life (whatever the hell that means).

But, first, a warning: Some of the material contained in these pages is not for the humoristically squeamish. If your refrigerator is currently covered with Family Circus or Nancy cartoons, it is suggested that you put this book down now. Many of these cartoons are ones my editors refused to run—others are ones I wish they hadn't. Either way, most people (with the exception of maybe a couple guys on Death Row) are bound to utter "Oh, my God" at least a few times during the course of this book.

The PreHistory of The Far Side is, among other things, an examination of what went wrong, what went right, and how rarely any two people seem to agree on which is which. (You can decide for yourself.)

As for the people who absolutely hate The Far Side, I have one thing to say: Your mother is a cow.

Part 1
Origin of the Species

THE FOSSIL RECORD

I loved to draw as a kid. But I need to emphasize that I never once thought about being a cartoonist. Likewise, I never studied art other than the required classes in grade school and junior high (to some people, that's immediately obvious). My love was science—specifically biology and, more specifically, when placed in a common jar, which of two organisms would devour the other.

Since The Far Side's story really begins in my childhood, I thought it might prove interesting to include a few of my earliest drawings. My mother was kind enough to provide a few of the things she saved from my kindergarten days, and I've provided a brief explanation (as best I can recall) of the catalyst for each one.

This was the house I grew up in. That's obviously my parents on the left and that's me looking out of my upstairs bedroom.

I made many drawings from this perspective. Apparently, it was the everyday view from my bedroom window.

Dinnertime in the Larson household. We were one of those close-knit families that considered the dinner hour an important aspect of family life.

My older brother and I used to play a lot of games together.

I loved Halloween as a kid. My parents loved it, too, and always insisted I be the same monster every year—something they called the "black ghost." What I've evidently drawn here is that very moment when the "black ghost" is ushered out the door to once again roam the streets and terrorize the neighborhood.

I remember quite fondly the games my mother used to play with me when I was growing up; such as one of my favorites (shown here) where she'd hide cookies from me and then give hints where I might find them.

I vividly remember playing with my dad and the dog in the backyard. The dog, as I recall, was not very fond of me.

In fact, this and other drawings like it are the only memories I have of our dog.

My dad used to love to make kids laugh. At the zoo, especially, he would sometimes incorporate my help to entertain whatever children were hanging around. I guess he wanted me to be popular.

My mom said that as soon as I'd get back from the zoo I'd run to my paper and crayons to try and draw whatever animals I saw that day. Drawings like this one represent some of my earliest impressions of wild creatures.

I believe this is my earliest memory of riding in the car when my family took our annual vacation.

One day, a long, long time ago at a retail music store where I had been working for almost a year, I had an unexpected revelation. As I stood next to the cash register, the sky seemed to suddenly open up over my head and a throng of beautiful angels came flying down and swirled around me. In glorious, lilting tones, their voices rang out, "you haaaaate your job, you haaaaate your job...." And then they left. But I knew it was true—angels don't lie. I hated my job.

There was nothing really that terrible about it but, without prior warning, it came over me that this just wasn't what I wanted out of life. (We didn't even get good employee discounts.) I wanted something more. Insurance salesman, ice cream vendor, gravedigger—many things occurred to me, but I was pretty much rudderless.

So I took a couple days off, went home, and thought about it. Of course, thinking about a career crisis for two whole days was more than my attention span could handle (a clue to why I do a single-panel cartoon instead of a strip), so I sat down at the kitchen table and started to draw. Exactly why, I'll never know. Other than an interest in *Mad* magazine during my adolescence, and an appreciation for Gahan Wilson's work in *Playboy*, I knew nothing about the cartooning world. But, on the other hand, cartooning is not exactly a field that requires a graduate degree, complete with upper division courses like "Noses 401" and "Crossed Eyes 502."

I gave it a whirl and drew a half-dozen cartoons. The net result was six of the worst little drawings cartoondom has ever seen. Baring my soul, here are five of the original six cartoons. (I couldn't find the sixth.)

"Yes... They're quite strange during the
larval stage."

"Vandalism!"

METAMORPHOSIS

The following day, I took these six little "gems" to a local magazine in Seattle called *Pacific Search* (now *Pacific Northwest*) and, amazingly enough, I hit paydirt. The editor liked them, and I received a ninety-dollar check. Immediately, I was surrounded by angels singing, "You looooove cartooning, you looooove cartooning...."

I quit my music store job and began drawing, living off a combination of a little money I had saved and my parents' gift of free room and board. And things started off great. I worked up a little creation called Nature's Way, a single-panel cartoon probably best described as a Mesozoic Far Side, and summed up the courage to show it to the editor of a small, weekly newspaper (the *Sumner News Review*). He liked it and began publishing it on a regular basis.

The sheer excitement of being published was enough to live on for a while, but the three bucks a cartoon I was getting began to have a sobering effect on my vision of doing this professionally. I'm not sure if it was the fear of rejection or what, but I effectively avoided knocking on other doors or submitting my work to various publishers. Eventually, I hung cartooning up and went out and got a "real" job—an investigator for the local Humane Society, to whom I never disclosed the fact that on the way to the job interview I ran over a dog.

Things went along for a while about as close to normal as my life had ever seemed and then, in 1979, a reporter I had met showed my cartoons to her editor at the *Seattle Times*. Nature's Way was resurrected and began appearing weekly in their Saturday edition—next to a kid's crossword puzzle called "Junior Jumble" (a hint that trouble was ahead). Some examples of these cartoons follow:

"He says it's for good luck."

"I just cleaned... so don't go dragging any slime in here!"

"Egad! What a hideous creature!"

"I believe we've been spotted."

"I hate to do this to you rats, but you give me no choice."

"This invention will change the course of man! I call it --- Hammer and Chisel!"

"Hey! What is this? I distinctly ordered the __steak__ sandwich."

"I'm sorry,... try the wizard up the road. I just used my last heart and brain."

"Bring back his ear."

"Last one out's a rotten egg!"

"O give me a home, Where the buffalo roam..."

"I don't think we're dealing here with your everyday locust swarm."

"Say, Frank. You don't happen to sleep with a teddy bear, do ya?"

"Of course I never eat the shells."

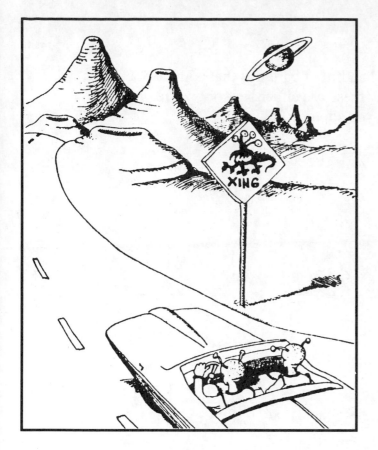

The Evolution of Modern Man

While working on Nature's Way, I drew a handful of cartoons that common sense dictated I never show anyone. If you think these are either sick or bizarre, you should have seen the ones I left out. (No, you shouldn't have.)

"Andrew is such a well-adjusted little boy... loves to work in the yard!"

Roses are red
Violets are blue
That's What They tell me
Because I'm Blind

"By God, Barnaby! Now there goes one big pigeon!"

After almost a year of this experience, with my confidence level high (I was back up to fifteen dollars per cartoon), I laid out a daring plan to expand this "publication empire": on my one week's vacation from the Humane Society I would take my portfolio and drive to San Francisco. With luck, I thought I had a chance at hooking up with another newspaper or magazine, thereby increasing my cartooning wages to, say, thirty bucks a week. But, all in all, the prime motivator was a shot at one simple goal: earning a living at something I enjoyed.

And so, in the summer of 1979, I jumped into my Plymouth Duster and headed south. I had with me a list of various publishers and their respective addresses, which I had gotten from the library, and into the "city by the bay" I drove.

My first target was the *San Francisco Chronicle,* primarily because I became lost in the city and found myself on Market Street, one of the names I recognized from my list. I found the building, parked the car, walked into the lobby with portfolio in hand, and came across a security guard who stopped me cold. Stupidly, I'd made no appointment, and I had no idea whom I should see on the subject of cartoons. I explained (lied) that I was a cartoonist for the *Seattle Times,* that I was in town just for the day, that I knew I was supposed to see someone about my work but I couldn't remember who, and anything else that came to mind. I guess I seemed convincingly more like a nerd than terrorist (who would have been better prepared), so he made a phone call and sent me up to another floor. And that's as far as I got. The receptionist politely told me that the cartoon editor was unavailable today, but that, if I wished, I could leave my portfolio with her and she would see that he would get it. As I handed it over, she added the encouraging words that the newspaper rarely bought features from "people who walked in off the street." I thanked her, left, and realized that I had just made a very major mistake: I had given her my one and only copy of my portfolio. It had completely escaped me that people might want to look at my drawings at a time that was convenient for them, and not for me.

For the next two days, "portfolioless," I hung around a telephone booth at Fisherman's Wharf. (I spent the night at the house of a friend who lived outside the city.) Every two or three hours I would call the receptionist at the *Chronicle* and inquire as to whether or not the cartoon editor had seen my work yet. The answer was always "no," and I remember becoming paranoid that she was getting progressively annoyed with me. Occasionally she would remind me "not to get my hopes up." They weren't, lady, they weren't.

I was screwed. During the day I had no place to stay (insert violin music) and I was very near the end of my vacation time. By the end of the second day of waiting to hear from the *Chronicle*, I made the decision to leave for home.

I called the receptionist for the last time. No, the editor had still not looked at my cartoons. Again, I thanked her, and headed for the *Chronicle* to retrieve my portfolio or to make arrangements for someone to forward it home. Either way, I was bummed, not so much because I realized what an idiot I was for trying such a harebrained scheme, or for the comedy of errors I made along the way, but mostly because I had just blown my one week's vacation time.

Before long, I was standing in front of the receptionist's desk for the second time in as many days. I told her who I was (she knew), and she said she would "ring Mr. Arnold." Obviously, I can't recall the exact details of the next events (although I'm close), but what stands out most vividly in my memory was the look of utter disbelief on this woman's face when she suddenly looked up at me and said, "Mr. Arnold would like to speak with you!"

Frankly, it scared the hell out of me as well. I took the receiver from her, and the voice at the other end said, "Are you Gary Larson?" I replied in the affirmative, and without hesitation, his next words were, "You're sick!" There was a brief pause (during which my stomach rolled into a granny knot), and then he quickly added, "I loved 'em!" Before we had said much more, he made a vague comment about syndication and then, unexpectedly, he asked, "Are you in the lobby?" I was in the lobby. "I'll come out and say hello. I'll be there in a couple of minutes."

I hung up, and the next thing I saw was the receptionist staring fixedly at me. She either asked or I told her that Mr. Arnold was coming out to the lobby. "He's coming out?" she exclaimed, and her expression of either shock or horror left me feeling like Fay Wray on the verge of a big meeting.

Stan Arnold was indeed a big man, but he was no Kong. He shook my hand and asked me to join him for a few minutes in his office. I did, and we chatted informally about cartoons and such for a while (my memory of this conversation is hazy—my brain was doing outside loops the whole time), and he ended up by asking me if I would mind leaving my portfolio with him for a few days (didn't I already do that?). He wanted to circulate it among some other editors. Finally, as he walked me back to the lobby, he added that, should the *Chronicle* indeed become interested in my work, one prospect would be syndication (something I knew nothing about). He would be in touch.

Back in the lobby, having already said goodbye to Stan and waiting for the elevator, I heard the sound of someone calling to me in a loud whisper. The receptionist was discreetly trying to flag me down, and at her signal I walked back to her desk. "I just wanted you to know that Mr. Arnold *never* comes out to the lobby for things like this! I've worked here ten years and I've never seen him do that! I just thought you'd like to know that he must think your work is very good." (Insert theme song from *Rocky* here.)

Man, my adrenal glands went into warp speed. I'm just lucky not to have been hit by a car as I walked out of the building. Of course, I didn't know what my chances were of any of this coming to fruition, but I sure felt a helluva lot better than I did an hour before.

Two days later, still on Cloud Nine, I arrived back home and found a letter in my mailbox from the *Seattle Times*. In essence, the brief message was a cancellation notice for Nature's Way. In the letter, Jim King, the managing editor, expressed his personal regret (he was always a fan) but explained that the cartoon had been generating just too many complaints and the editorial consensus was to terminate it. (I *knew* it shouldn't have been next to "Junior Jumble.")

The timing of all this has always fascinated me. As I stated earlier, I had never been very aggressive about pushing my work initially and my "in" with the *Seattle Times* had been very motivational. I'll always be convinced that, had the *Times* mailed that letter out a week earlier, I never would have made the trip to San Francisco. The wind would definitely have gone out of my sails.

The next day I got a phone call from Stan Arnold. Chronicle Features, the syndicate affiliate of the *San Francisco Chronicle*, had indeed decided to syndicate my work and would be sending a contract to me shortly. In addition, he said they had decided to call it The Far Side, if that was okay with me. It was okay with me. (They could have called it "Revenge of the Zucchini People" for all I cared.)

On January 1, 1980, a single-panel cartoon called The Far Side debuted in the *San Francisco Chronicle*, and several months later, Chronicle Features began officially offering it to other newspapers.

Two years later, Andrews and McMeel, the publishing arm of another syndicate—Universal—brought out my first book, also called *The Far Side*. Very much to my own surprise, and the collective shock of decent, Garfield-loving people everywhere, it became a successful publication. It seemed natural, then, when my first contract expired in 1984, to move to Andrews and McMeel's parent company Universal Press Syndicate.

That's the story. Of course, I don't know how interesting any of this really is, but now you've got it in your brain cells so you're stuck with it.

Part 2
Evolution...

CREATIVE PROCESS

"Where do you get your ideas?" has always been the question I'm most often confronted with. ("*Why* do you get your ideas?" is a close second.) I've always found the question interesting, because it seems to embody a belief that there exists some secret, tangible place of origin for cartoon ideas. Every time I hear it, I'm struck by this mental image where I see myself rummaging through my grandparents' attic and coming across some old, musty trunk. Inside, I find this equally old and elegant-looking book. I take it in my hands, blow away the dust, and embossed on the front cover in large, gold script is the title, *Five Thousand and One Weird Cartoon Ideas*.

I'm afraid the real answer is much more mundane: I don't know where my ideas come from. I will admit, however, that one key ingredient is caffeine. I get a couple cups of coffee into me and things just start to happen.

The idea for any cartoon (my experience, anyway) is rarely spontaneous. Good ideas usually evolve out of pretty lame ones, and vice versa. (I've destroyed a few good cartoons by reworking them to death.) There's only one cartoon idea I ever got that came directly from my own personal experience, and this is it:

And some of my cartoons (some would argue most), I realize, are not always understandable. I mean, I know what I was going for—I just have to face the fact that I don't always quite get there. "Off days" are a part of life, I guess, whether you're a cartoonist, a neurosurgeon, or an air-traffic controller.

Nevertheless, I thought it might be interesting (if not embarrassing) to include a section in this book with excerpts from my sketchbook—some that eventually became Far Side cartoons, and some miscellaneous doodles, short stories, anecdotes, etc. I've also included some examples of problems I've encountered in my efforts to publish my cartoons once they've been created.

Some cartoons spring forth from just staring stupidly at a blank sheet of paper and thinking about aardvarks or toaster ovens or cemeteries or just about anything, and others come out of "doodles" that I continually enter into a sketchbook. On the following pages are some of these sketchbook "doodles" and writings from my sketchbook. In some cases I've included the final rendition that became a Far Side panel. Other things are just nonsensical, inane little drawings that have no bearing on anything whatsoever, but for some unknown reason they came out of me so here they are.

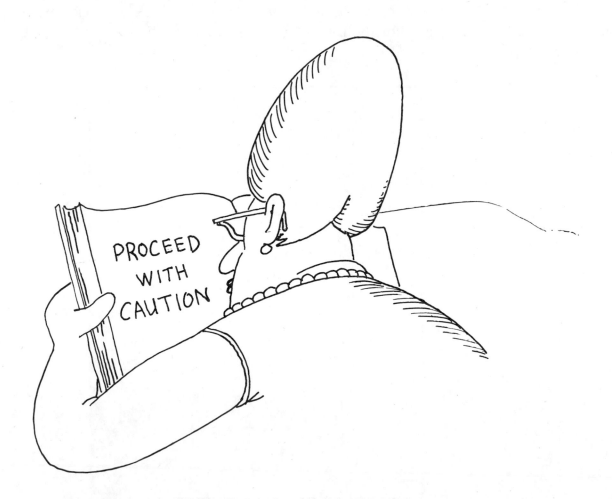

The burglars surrendered
at the sight of looking down
Harold's Dobermann gun.
Dobie-o-matic.

1985

Suddenly the burglars found themselves looking down the
barrel of Andy's Dobie-o-matic.

When an idea hits, it's important for me to write it down or sketch it as quickly as possible. (I've lost more than one cartoon idea because I thought I could remember it later.) Leafing through my sketchbook, I was surprised to find this Doberman "gun" idea which sparked the "Dobie-o-matic" cartoon.

"I'm sorry about this, ma'am, but his license all checks out... but maybe I can get him to take your husband somewhere else and clean him."

I decided the caption on the first draft was just too graphic and unsettling (although it's what deer hunters do, isn't it?), and I modified it in the final version.

"I'm sorry, ma'am, but his license does check out and, after all, your husband *was* in season. Remember, just because he knocks doesn't mean you have to let him in."

Down at the Eat and Slither

The first version of this (upper) seemed just a tad grotesque, and I ended up eliminating the pig being swallowed. (On another note, I'm not exactly sure how these snakes are holding up their newspapers.)

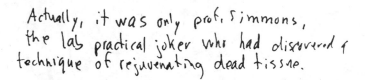

Actually, it was only prof. Simmons,
the lab practical joker who had discovered a
technique of rejuvenating dead tissue.

*I have absolutely no idea what the little doodle above
means or where it came from, but it led to this Far Side.
(And now I know where the latter came from, but I still
don't know what it means.)*

Scene from *Return of the Nose of Dr. Verlucci*

"So, Professor Jenkins!...My old nemesis!...We meet again, but this time the advantage is mine! Ha! Ha! Ha!"

What kind of a sordid, bizarre past a scientist and some duck could possibly have is for anyone to surmise, but I enjoyed the drama in suggesting that, once again, their lives have become entangled and a new chapter is about to be written. Personally, I enjoy cartoons of this type because they lack the obvious "cymbal crash" at the end of the punch line. The idea evolved as shown.

"I'm leaving you, Harry... and I'm taking the maggots with me."

Above is my first version of this idea, but this is one of those rare instances when even I found something sort of repugnant in the drawing. The grubs (right) just seemed more palatable (not in the edible sense).

"I'm leaving you, Charles... and I'm taking the grubs with me."

"Uh-oh. Guess what I've got to do again?...
Could you please stop at someone's living room?"

"Oh yeah? Well, If I was driving, I'd
probably go about a hundred miles an hour."

"Think about it, Murray....If we could get this baby runnin',
we could run over hikers, pick up females, chase down mule
deer — man, we'd be the grizzlies from hell."

*For me, the caption (if there is one) and the drawing
are a simultaneous concept. In this case, however, I
knew these bears would be pretty excited about their
"find" but it took some time to decide how best to
express it.*

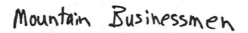
Mountain Businessmen

I just started thinking about mountain men and the wild frontier and Jeremiah Johnson and before long out came Seymour.

1985

Seymour Frishberg: Accountant of the Wild Frontier

Nerd sharks always ran the projector

1985

Shark nerds always ran the projector.

Sometimes I feel like the rough sketches I do of certain cartoons capture something more interesting than the ones that are worked up. The crude but loose feeling in the quick sketch of this cartoon is, to my eye, more successful than the final.

The deer, I think, is any one of us caught in the situation where some maniac, having entered our home, is trying to hunt us down and kill us. (Pleasant thought—I wonder if Ernie Bushmiller ever worked with this theme in Nancy.) I started with the "horrible movie" idea but decided it didn't make much sense compared to the deer simply trying to collect himself.

Faith Surgeons

Faith Repairmen
Faith Repairers
Instrument healers
Appliance healers

Appliance healers

I started thinking about faith healers one day and how much obvious humor potential just exuded from these people. I played with these two versions before ending up with the final, as shown.

53

Suddenly, professor Leibowitz realized he had come to the seminar without his duck.

In this cartoon, I tried to tap into that universal fear I think we all have of being blatantly unprepared for some important, purposeful gathering like those dreams of going to school or work in just your underwear. But to forget your duck, *of course,* means you're really screwed.

Suddenly, Professor Liebowitz realizes he has come to the seminar without his duck.

"Well, of *course* I did it in cold blood, you idiot!...I'm a reptile!"

This idea didn't change much between the sketch and the final drawing, except I decided the attorney in this case was definitely an idiot, not a nerd. (These are important considerations.)

I once referred to a character in one of my cartoons as a "dork" (a popular insult when I was growing up), but my editor called me up and said that "dork" couldn't be used because it meant "penis." I couldn't believe it. I ran to my New Dictionary of American Slang *and, sure enough, he was right. All those years of saying or being called a "dork" and I had never really known what it meant. What a nerd.*

Boy, there's no love-loss there... That cat never has ~~figured out exactly what~~ forgiven ~~a goddam cat~~ that piranha.

I was playing around with the caption on this cartoon before it suddenly dawned on me that it really didn't need one. The story's told by just the scene of a legless cat in a store with a piranha residing nearby in a fishbowl. I also decided to put wooden legs on the cat in the final version, not wanting to make cat fanciers more upset than necessary.

Aquarists, however, loved it.

Working on the Beaten Path

"I don't know if this is such a wise thing to do, George."

The idea came in up above and came out on the bottom cartoon.

The original and unpublished version of this is shown on the top. I'm unclear as to why I changed it. Looking at it now, I may have made the wrong decision. Naaaaaah.

My brother once woke up screaming in the middle of the night from a nightmare. In his dream, a wolf, with "pure, white eyes" and walking on its hind legs, was trying to get him. He was able to quickly dismiss the ordeal, but he told the story so vividly that his younger sibling (me) could never shake the image. Ironically, my brother's nightmare ended up scaring me for years. The creature on the right in this cartoon closely resembles the "wolf" as I've always pictured it.

In bed at night, I was so scared of this and other monsters that I nearly suffocated trying to stay completely under the blankets. Any exposed skin meant certain death.

The monster snorkel would have been a wonderful thing in my little world. (It still would be.)

The monster snorkel: Allows your child to breathe comfortably without exposing vulnerable parts to an attack.

Inevitably, their affair ended: Howard worried excessively about what the pack would think, and Agnes simply ate the flowers.

Originally, the title I intended for this cartoon was, simply, "Predator/prey relationships." But when I finished the drawing, something about the way the wolf was looking back over his shoulder evoked a need in me to probe their relationship a little deeper.

59

Every time that I've seen a stuffed bear, it's posed in the standard, threatening-like stance. I guess every bear hunter would like to give the impression that this is exactly how the animal was snuffed—seconds before he (the hunter) was to be pulled into that terrible maw.

I think the truth is much more akin to what I've drawn here.

A friend and I were walking across the zoo grounds one day when another friend, an employee of the zoo, began to scream at us from afar, "Riffraff in the zoo! Riffraff in the zoo!"
   Voila!

"Yes, they're all fools, gentlemen... But the question remains, what kind of fools are they?"

1983

"Yes, they're all fools, gentlemen.... But the question remains,
'What *kind* of fools are they?'"

*I got lucky on this one. The first version seemed to be
exactly what I was looking for, and very little had to be
changed in the final. (I know most of those people
behind the glass.)*

*"Nice threads" led to this cartoon. Or maybe it didn't.
I can't remember but if it had it would have been
interesting.*

"You and Fred have such a lovely web, Edna — and I *love*
what you've done with those fly wings."

If Dogs Drove

On the Dog Bus

Apparently this was a little confusing to some people. I just meant if dogs drove or commuted to work on the bus or whatever, they'd most likely hang their heads out the window. That's it. No big deal. (I now think the whole thing would have been improved by changing the caption to, "Dogs on their way to work." Oh, well.)

1988   Larson

When dogs go to work

63

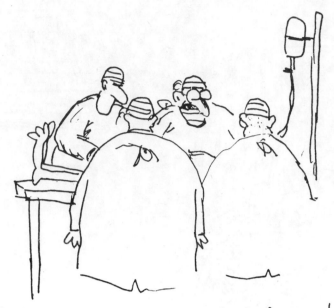

Man, this is weird... Halfway in to this operation, and I've just drawn a total blank on procedure... In fact, I think I'm an ice cream man.

1984   Larson

"OK, Wellington. I'm comfortable with my grip if you are....
Have you made a wish?"

I have no idea what the uppermost sketch means. In fact, I can't say for sure if these cartoons were part of the same creative process or not. So, I won't comment about that—but I'd just like to say that these are some of the fattest doctors I think I've drawn.

In an effort to be friendly, Elroy is instantly vaporized when he grabs one of the creatures by the head and shakes vigorously.

Inadvertently, Roy dooms the entire earth to annihilation when, in an attempt to be friendly, he seizes their leader by the head and shakes vigorously.

The first version of this seemed, well—wrong. I decided the farmer had to be in the cartoon to make it a little more understandable—but it's a weird cartoon no matter how you look at it.

Eons ago, shortly before my first blind date, my dad gave me the worst haircut of my life. At a time when longer hair was cool, I ended up looking like a character on a join-the-army poster.

This sketch and final cartoon are directly related to that mortifying experience and indelible memory. (Around last summer, I forgave my dad.)

"Oh, and here's Luanne now. ... Bobby just got sheared today, Luanne."

"You wanna have to use your brain your whole life like me? No kid of mine's going thru that hell... Here, learn to dribble this thing."

Einstein and son

1987 Larson

Unbeknownst to most historians, Einstein started down the road of professional basketball before an ankle injury diverted him into science.

I still sort of prefer the first sketch I made of this, but, for one reason or another, I changed it to the bottom version.

I felt like the first version of this was actually better, in the sense that, if the adult Grim Reaper carries a sickle, then as a kid he must have carried scissors. I worried about it for some reason and ended up changing it to the bottom version.

1986

The Grim Reaper as a child

1986

"Well, one guess which table wants another round of banana daiquiris."

After completing this cartoon, I realized one of the apes had to be sucking an empty glass onto his face (as I myself used to be quite good at), so it was necessary to start over.

"A bald head, Murray! A bald head!.. And it's right-under-neath-me!.."

How birds see the world.

It wasn't difficult to go from the sketch above to the final version. After all, I believe this is true.

"Oh, for heaven's sake, Miss Carlisle!... They're
only cartoon animals!"

*I've discovered an interesting phenomenon. Once
you've drawn Rocky the Flying Squirrel, you can never
draw him again. In the final version, I must have drawn
and erased that miserable little rodent fifty times, and
he ultimately ended up looking like Rocky the Flying
Hamster.*

"For crying out loud, Doris. ... You gotta drag that thing out *every* time we all get together?"

Whenever and wherever my family gets together for a big dinner, my mother (whose name is Doris) feels compelled to pull out her camera and take the quintessential shot of the Larsons about to bolt down their meal.

Since wolves are such social animals, it was an easy jump in my mind to go from a wolf-kill to a Larson meal.

Edgar finds his purpose.

A friend of mine related a story of how she once brought a boyfriend of hers to her parents' house for dinner. Her father and her boyfriend (Edgar) apparently didn't hit it off real well, and before the evening was over, her father ended up saying to Edgar, "You know what your problem is, don't you? Your problem is you don't have a purpose! Everyone has to have a purpose in life, and you simply haven't found one!"

I have no idea if the real Edgar ever found his purpose or not, but if he did, this is how I imagined it.

"When I'm in my own yard I feel invicible, doc... Step outside and, poof! No confidence"

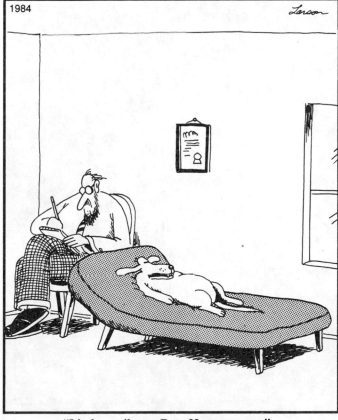

1984   Larson

"It's the mailman, Doc. He scares me."

I hate the cartoon cliché of someone (or, in my case, some animal) on a psychiatrist's couch. I'll do them, obviously, but for some reason this situation always points out the lunacy of mixing animal and human behavior. If the psychiatrist was also a dog, I'd be more comfortable with it. But the approach I've used here makes me want to say, "Wait a minute—dogs don't visit psychiatrists! How'd he even find the right floor?" Before long, I start analyzing the improbabilities in everything I've drawn and I might end up having to lie down on the couch for a while.

"Uh-oh...He's using the thingy."

"So! Still won't talk?...I guess it's time to use a little device we (like to) call around here 'the thingy.'"

This cartoon developed as shown, and I was satisfied with the final—except to say I'm always worried some people will try to figure out what exactly it is that the "Mr. Thingy" does. (I'm sure this is residual paranoia from the "Cow tools" cartoon, see page 156.)

1984

"Well, we've tried every device and you still won't talk — every device, that is, except this little baby we simply call 'Mr. Thingy.'"

This idea, exactly as I had sketched it in the version below, sat around for months before I actually tried it out in The Far Side. It seemed to go over well, from what I heard, but mostly with guys named "Doug."

"Raised the ol' girl from a cub, I did. ...'Course, we had to get a few things straight between us. She don't try to follow me into town anymore, and I don't try and take her food bowl away 'til she's done."

The most loving, gregarious dogs seem to get down to their basic instincts pretty fast when you reach for their food bowl midmeal. (For a real thrill, try reaching for it in slow motion. Dogs love *the sensation that their food is being stalked.)*

I started playing with this tendency in dogs, and it just sort of evolved into the grizzly bear cartoon seen at left.

75

The spitting cobras at home

The cartoon potential on the subject of spitting cobras is enormous. People have asked me if I ever worry about running out of ideas for cartoons, but I think the array of nature's creatures that sting, bite, spit, stab, suck, gore, or stomp is just about endless. I never worry.

say it, don't spray it, al

Why spitting cobras don't have friends

Practical jokes of the wild

After completing this cartoon in the "deer" version, it just didn't click with me, humorwise. I tried it again with bears, and I suppose, because of their ability to stand on their hind legs, they more closely approximate a group of guys standing around doing the same thing—and, to my eye, making it more effective.

Practical jokes of the wild

76

It seems to me that every time I watch a nature show about lions, I hear something like this: "...and with jaws that can crush the bones of a buffalo, the mother lion gently lifts her little cub and carries it to blah blah blah..."

I had to try to capture something of that phrase in a cartoon.

"Oo, Sylvia! You've got to see this!... Ginger's bringing Bobby home, and even though her jaws can crush soup bones, Bobby only gets a few nicks and scratches."

"Oo! Goldfish, everyone! Goldfish!"

I've always been drawn to swamps and wetlands and the things that live there. In those places, I find myself mostly looking downward for frogs, fish, salamanders, or whatever.

I think if I ever lived in feudal times and stormed past a castle gate, I'd have to check out the moat on the way across.

I suppose I like this cartoon not only for the suggestion that the usual crocodiles have been replaced with goldfish, but because that's me yelling on the bridge.

"Fire!"

1984

I've lost track of Mad magazine over the years, but as a teenager I really enjoyed it. I think this Far Side cartoon reflects a definite Mad influence.

When I was a kid, it seemed to me that my dad was constantly out in the garage working on some mechanical project. I was his gofer on these projects, and I especially remember the pressure of being asked to fetch a specific-size wrench.

In the corner of his shop was a huge steel cabinet with assorted drawers, one of which contained about six thousand wrenches. The sizes on these grease-covered tools were sometimes difficult to read, and it was always with an edge of trepidation that I would hand him one. My dad, however, through some mystery of nature, always knew exactly what size he needed for the job at hand. It only took him a nanosecond to say, "Nope, that's not it."

I started thinking about those famous "bolts" in the neck of Frankenstein's monster (in fact, I've often pondered them), and that in turn sparked the memory of those stormy lightning-filled nights when my dad, with his own little Igor, tried to bring life to a dead lawnmower.

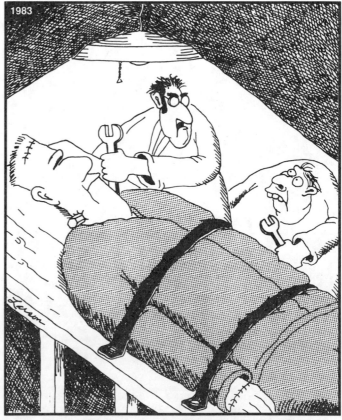

"Fool! This is an eleven-sixteenths...I asked for a five-eighths!"

78

A cartoon inspired by the memory of a classmate of mine in junior high—I think he's a senator now.

"Well, I've got your final grades ready, although I'm afraid not everyone here will be moving up."

"Henry! Hurry or you're gonna miss it — ghost riders in the kitchen!"

Sometimes, when you stay up too late at night trying to think of something funny, these things happen. Except to say that it's obviously inspired by "Ghost Riders in the Sky," I haven't the slightest idea what "Ghost Riders in the Kitchen" means. I'll figure it out one day. (I should have followed up the next day with "Ghost Riders in the Living Room.")

79

Channel 42 — your vampire station

In hindsight, I wish I hadn't included the title to this vampire cartoon. It's obviously redundant and only distracted from the humor.

Primitive humor

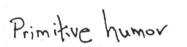

Humor at its lowest form

"Did I say you could come up?.. Did@. I @! !!"

"I built the forms around him just yesterday afternoon when he fell asleep, and by early evening I was able to mix and pour."

"Yeah. My boss don't appreciate me either. To him I'm just a gofer. 'Igor! Go for brains!…Igor! Go for dead bodies…Igor! Go for sandwiches!'…I dunno — give me another beer."

"I work for this scientist… I dig up graves, fetch brains, mop the floor — general stuff… you wanna see the lab? blah blah blah —— So And you?"

"With feeling, Russel – with feeling!"...

Another little "slice of life" scene. The rough sketch evoked something in me (more successfully than the final, I think) and I just ended up drawing it.

"Blow, Howie, blow!... Yeah, yeah, yeah! You're cookin' now, Howie!... All right!... Charlie Parker, move over!... Yeah!"

" Egad... ~~My Kerchief~~ My monogramed ~~han~~ handkerchief! I've left it behind... They'll know it was me!

1984

"Take this handkerchief back to the lab, Stevens. I want some answers on which monster did this — Godzilla! Gargantua! Who?"

I changed my mind about the approach to this cartoon and drew it instead from the perspective of the police. And the only name I could think of for the handkerchief was King Kong. There just aren't too many famous monsters running around with first and last names.

This idea first centered around a snake taking a shower, its "robe" thrown on the bathroom floor. That image, in turn, sparked the idea for a swimming hole scene, in which the respective worlds of man and snake collide.

"Hors d'oeuvre?"

Something about the porcupine sketch above makes me now prefer it to the final version, although I have no idea why.

"Look at that... Man, in our day, Bernie, we could skeletonize a cow in less than two minutes."

Just about every time I've heard or read anything about piranhas (as you might imagine, I'm drawn to the subject), it's always mentioned how quickly a school of them can skeletonize a cow. I'm not sure why a cow is always the standard unit of measurement for this sort of thing, but pondering it eventually led to this cartoon.

"Hold up, Niles. It says here, 'These little fish have been known to skeletonize a cow in less than two minutes.'... Now *there's* a vivid thought."

"Sometimes I think you've got a brain the size of a walnut."

"The picture's pretty bleak, gentlemen.... The world's climates are changing, the mammals are taking over, and we all have a brain about the size of a walnut."

"I've seen this before, Jackson... And it's not a pretty sight."

I won't go into the bizarre details, but I once had a close call involving a rather large Burmese python that I had raised from a baby (the snake). By the time I awakened to the fact that, instead of an interesting and beautiful member of the reptile family, I was now living with a gigantic predator with a very small brain (the snake), one day she attempted to do me in. (I'm sure that's how a lot of people would expect me to check out, anyway.)

Before and after my own little episode, I've heard stories of other people getting croaked in their apartments by events you normally associate with the jungle.

I got rid of the snake, and in so doing improved not only my chances of living awhile longer but my social life as well.

"I've seen this sort of thing before, Baxter... and it's *not* a pretty sight."

"Oooooo!.. Mr. Van Horn!... The duck is back -- staring at your back."

Raymond could feel it... First a tingling at the base of his neck and then a cold sweat would quickly engulf his body -- yes, the duck was staring at him again.

1988

Larson

Anatidaephobia: The fear that somewhere, somehow, a duck is watching you.

Another example of perhaps overworking a cartoon. In hindsight, I wish I had used the final drawing but with the second caption in the sketch above, which begins, "Raymond could feel it..." It just seems a little more interesting to me.

In coming up with the name for the phobia, I played around with words like "quackaphobia" and "duckalookaphobia" and so on. But then I got the bright idea to look up the scientific name for ducks, and discovered their family name is Anatidae. And so, I ended up coining a word that twelve ornithologists understood and everyone else probably went, "Say what?"

Street physicians

This is perhaps a good example of how I'll break a mental block (other than getting out my contract and rereading it). I scribbled out this strange little street musician, hoping to get something happening. It started me thinking about mimes, jugglers, and other street performers—and the possibility of other professions moving into the same scene.

Street physicians

I don't think this ever really worked. The title on the dog's book is a well-known phrase, but I couldn't recall any expressions that would similarly reflect a cat's reading interests. In cases like this, I usually sit on the idea with the hope that someday I'll stumble across it in my sketchbook and immediately know how to handle it. This time, unfortunately, I think I forced it.

"Mr. Bailey? There's a gentleman here who claims an ancestor of yours once defiled his crypt, and now you're the last remaining Bailey and…oh, something about a curse. Should I send him in?"

91

Early American Cow Dance

"Oh! *Four* steps to the left and *then* three to the right!... What
kind of a dance was *I* doing?"

"You know, we could really use a spatula."

"Man, this is our lucky day, Bob... Smashed bacon & eggs on the road."

Secret tools of the common crow

A strategy for survival used by some spiders is known as "ballooning." Baby spiders crawl out on a leaf or something and cast out a long, secreted thread that, catching a breeze, carries them aloft to far and distant lands. I started thinking about the phenomenon of "ballooning" in spiders (someone has to) and I just sort of doodled out a literal translation of its meaning. Eventually, it occurred to me that, within the confines of The Far Side, there may be other animals that employ the same tactic. Why, bison, of course.

Spiders ballooning

More Facts of Nature: As part of nature's way to help spread the species throughout their ecological niche, bison often utilize a behavior naturalists have described as "ballooning."

Thwarting the vampcow

Thwarting the vamprow

Vamprow

95

The seed for this cartoon all started with a simple T-shirt design. If T-shirts were as popular in the nineteenth century as they are today, I wondered what kinds of things they would say. The sketch above led to this cartoon.

When I was a kid, I often listened to my grandfather sing a song that started off with the words, "Buffalo Gal won't you come out tonight, come out tonight, come out tonight [repeats]...and we'll dance by the light of the moon."

I realize now that I never understood what a "Buffalo Gal" was. My image was someone who looked a lot like the woman in this cartoon.

It was inevitable, therefore, that she one day meet the Elephant Man.

The Elephant Man meets a Buffalo Gal

1987

The elephant man meets the buffalo gal.

1980

"We've still got a couple of years to go before we're ready for the moon."

It all started innocently enough. I hadn't thought much about cows in my entire life. They were nice animals, both on and off the dinner table. And that about sums up my attitude toward them. And then it happened.

In May of 1980, I drew the cartoon at left. When I finished, I sat back and stared at my little creation. Something moved me. This was more than just a cow—this was an entire career I was looking at. As the following pages indicate, I should have just called this thing The Cow Side and forgot about it.

SKETCHBOOK SAMPLER

Late at night, as I'm working at my drafting table, mental fatigue starts to take over. The problem is, it takes me awhile to figure out that this is happening. And so I sometimes keep right on drawing until, eventually, I realize it's becoming difficult to erase because of the proximity of my nose to the paper.

At those times I draw some pretty weird things in my sketchbook. I'm not saying *funny*, I'm saying *weird*. These are things that I look at the next day and wonder what in the hell I was thinking about. (As if I know at the other times.)

I'm not entirely sure of the wisdom in this, but I thought I'd take some of these little cartoon "musings" and throw them in this book. Regardless of what interpretations or reactions they may elicit, I can assure you they are entirely meaningless. Anyone who attaches more significance to them needs to get out more often.

"Hello, Margo... I've brought you some chocolate-covered fish-heads."

Spider bars

Down at the ant pizza-parlor

Atilla the Bun.

Unwittingly, Vicky flirts with Death

Gus buys the wrong cat food

I wonder what time it is...I feel like I've been dead for three days.

Jesus rises from the grave

My apologies if half the world takes offense at this. I'm not antireligious or anti-Christian (I'm a little cynical about TV evangelists). I just can't help thinking about things like this and what it would feel like to anybody to get up after that long in the netherworld.

Evolution of the Nerd

"The vet let me keep them...
they're my testicles."

"Slither softy but carry a lot of venom."

"I never met a man I didn't bite"

"Sting first, ash questions later."

"A swimmer in the water is worth two on the beach."

I was going to do a cartoon that was a collage of various animals and their favorite sayings—but I never did. I drew these four and got stuck.

Dung Scientists

Hello, brethren!

Uh-oh.. Quackers!

Wolf in ~~sheep~~ clothing.
tacky

Modern
Stampede

109

110

Bad chickens

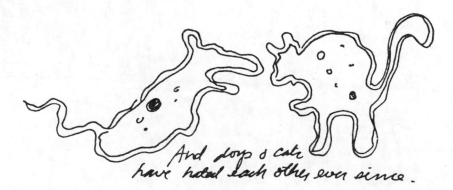

And dogs & cats
have hated each other ever since.

STORIES

Sometimes ideas have come out of short stories or ramblings I write just to shift gears once in a while. Cartoons are, after all, little stories themselves, frozen at an interesting point in time. What follows are several stories that either led to cartoons, could have led to cartoons, or were just ideas in and of themselves.

PHILOSOPHY

Professor Irwin Schwartz was on his way to give a lecture based on his latest book, *Mind Over Matter*, when his car failed to negotiate a curve, plummeted over the embankment, rolled end to end across the boulders, and finally burst into flames.

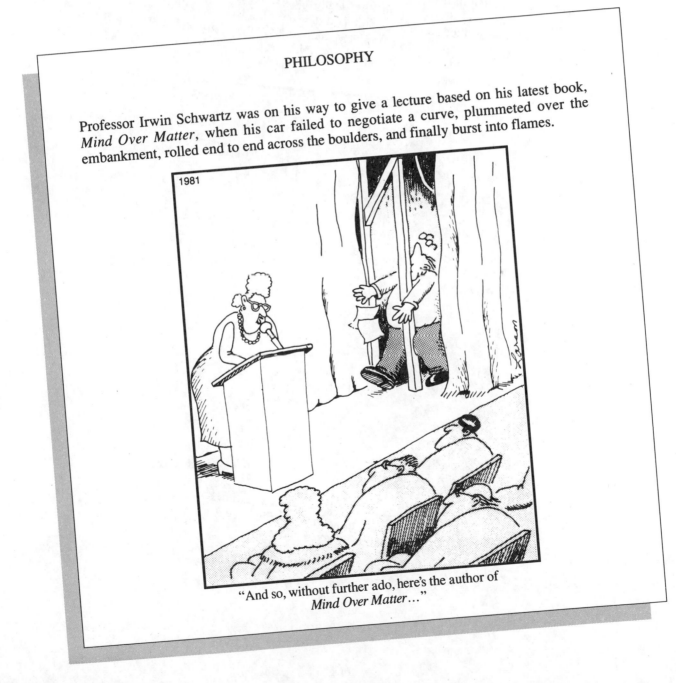

"And so, without further ado, here's the author of *Mind Over Matter*..."

THE CLASS PROJECT

We had designed the robot in metal shop to do peaceful functions and serve mankind. Mr. Rockford supervised the project but mostly he just read his magazines and swore at us for screwing around excessively.

As the semester waned, a few of us who were hoping to get an "A" became concerned that the robot may indeed not be completed in time. Subsequently, we all agreed to start showing up during study hall and after school to work on the thing.

Without supervision, however, things gradually got out of hand. I think it was Randy Boone who suggested inserting the death-ray. It went on from there as we constructed the steel-toothed mandibles and a double-barreled flamethrower.

Weeks later, our creation was completed and we activated it for the first time at an assembly in front of the entire student body. Needless to say, when the carnage finally ended, we all received an "F."

"My project's ready for grading, Mr. Big Nose.... Hey! I'm talkin' to *you*, squidbrain!"

THE FRIDGE

I was standing in the kitchen one day, fixing a sandwich or something, when suddenly I heard a very distinct "sneeze" emanate from the fridge. Naturally curious, I opened the door and scrutinized the various food items. Suddenly, the mayonnaise began to scream, "The ketchup did it! The ketchup!"

Of course, I was stunned. This, after all, was an inanimate object. And, truthfully, to this very day, I've never been able to coax the ketchup to say or do anything and have concluded the sneeze was my own imagination.

"I'll just take *this*, thank you! ... And knock off that music!"

BOBBY

Tired of being forced to eat his oatmeal, Bobby decided to run away from home as far as he could get. And he made excellent progress—until some Masai warriors found him and called his parents.

"Mrs. Harriet Schwartz? This is Zathu Nananga of the Masai....Are you missing a little boy?"

ZOOLOGY

The bear and Carl lived together in the cave for several years until, one day, the true savagery of Nature being unleashed, Carl killed and ate him.

THE WRONG NUMBER

Larry lived alone in his small inner-city apartment. He had no friends and most people ignored him at all costs.

Then one day, unexpectedly, the phone rang. And Larry was surprised to find himself talking to God.

"Is this 555-3178?" God asked.

"No, this is 555-7138."

"Sorry." And God hung up.

ALIENS

When the aliens arrived none of us were ready. We were sitting around the dinner table, mindlessly chattering, when the knock came. Aunt Rose went to the door, swung it open, and was instantly vaporized. Horrified, we watched Aunt Rose's ashes slowly settle to the floor. The door creaked shut. "Aliens!" Grandma whispered.

A few moments of silence followed. And then the knock returned. This time Grandma grabbed her shotgun, signaled everyone of her intent, and crept quietly to the door. The kind, eternal light had left her blue eyes. Her jaw was set, and I saw the look of the vengeful she-wolf bent on protecting her cubs.

Grandma suddenly flung the door open and I saw her pump two rounds into Harold Schmidt, the grocer up the street. When the smoke cleared, we all stood there—quietly observing Harold's twisted, broken body.

"Who would have thought?" Grandma's voice quivered. "Old Harold Schmidt—a stinkin' alien!"

PALEONTOLOGY

It was a beautiful day for a picnic and the Anderson family was taking full advantage. They had just laid the blanket down and were getting out the potato salad when one of the kids began to scream. Within seconds the once peaceful air was filled with shrieks and bellows and, before long, the entire Anderson family was sucked down into the tarpits where they joined the mammoth, the woolly rhinoceros, and the Stevens family from the week before.

Part 3
Mutations...

MISTAKES
(MINE AND THEIRS)

Nothing is perhaps more frustrating in this business than to open a newspaper, turn to the comic page, glance nonchalantly at your own little creation and discover that some behind-the-scenes *idiot* has screwed it all up.

No, strike that. Nothing is perhaps more frustrating in this business than to open a newspaper, turn to your own little creation, and discover that some idiot has screwed it all up, and discover that that idiot was *you*.

Between the time an idea for a cartoon gets conceived in my head and the day it's actually published in any given newspaper, a lot can go awry. It might be a basic flaw in the cartoon's premise, a word or two deleted by a typesetter, or the entirely wrong caption set to the wrong cartoon.

Whatever, it's just so much *fun* when these things happen.

In my first year or so of drawing The Far Side, I was scared to death of making mistakes in the artwork. Incredibly, I had never heard of a product called "White Out" (for covering up mistakes) and the smallest screw-up meant starting over. So, as I've indicated under each of these cartoons, I sometimes left things out.

1980

"And so I ask the jury...is that the face of a mass murderer?"

This is interesting. I have no idea where this guy's legs are.

1980

1980

"Next!"

The fellow coming through the door is incompletely drawn because I feared the lines of his body would interfere with the auditioner's head. Obviously, I choked.

CYMBAL AUDITIONS

"And this must be the little woman."

I hate drawing this type of rug because I can never seem to make the concentric circles come out right. I'd get halfway, as shown, and quit.

122

Sled Chickens of the North

"That does it, Sid.... You yell 'tarantula' one more time and you're gonna be wearin' this thing."

"Sled Chickens of the North" was published with just one minor flaw—the chickens weren't harnessed to anything. They're just running along, no "strings" attached. Oh, well.

As a reader pointed out to me, bananas don't grow this way. The individual bananas grow upward, not downward (as I've drawn them here).

One side of me wants to say, "So sue me," but the truth is, it does bug me when I make these kinds of mistakes.

123

"And now Edgar's gone....Something's going on
around here."

Over the years, The Far Side has cultivated a following
among some scientists. And, of course, I've found that
especially flattering—but it does have its downside. A
certain degree of accuracy is expected from these folks.

After this "polar bear" cartoon was published, I
received letters from several biologists reminding me
that polar bears are strictly an Arctic species, and
penguins strictly Antarctic. Damn.

And I really heard it when this "mosquito" cartoon
came out. Numerous readers wrote to remind me that
it's the female that does the biting, not the male. I knew
that. (Of course, it's perfectly acceptable that these
creatures wear clothes, live in houses, speak English,
etc.)

"What a day....I must have spread malaria across
half the country."

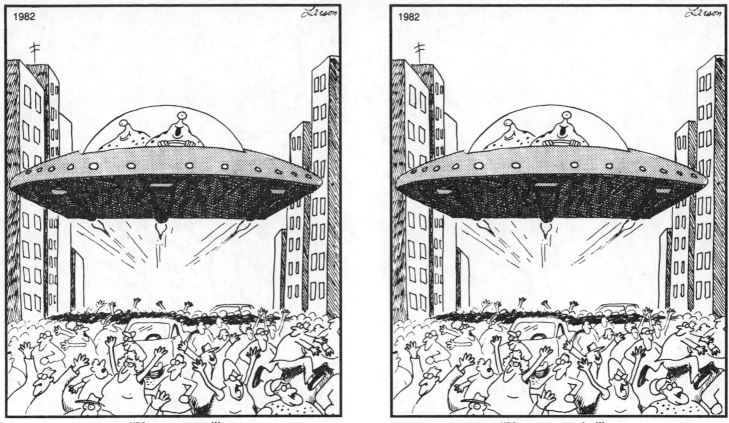

"Yeeeeeeeeeee!"   "Yeeeeeeeeeeeha!"

The Far Side starts off being drawn in a 6" x 7.5" size. In pencil, I rough in and then refine the image until it fairly closely approximates what's in my head. (That's a scary thought.) Inking and shading are my last steps. The caption is handwritten in pencil in the area where it would normally appear. When the syndicate receives this original, the caption is set into its usual typeface, the copyright and publication date are added, and the whole thing is reduced down to the size normally seen in newspapers. Six of these "ready-to-go" cartoons are compiled into a mailer representing one week's worth of material, and then shipped to newspaper clients a few weeks in advance of their usage.

I receive the mailers as well, and the day this cartoon showed up I was horrified to see that the last two letters in the caption had been deleted. Instead of "Yeeeeeeeeha," it read "Yeeeeeeeeee." Someone at the syndicate had screwed up.

Obviously, this small error had a significant impact on the feel of the cartoon. But I hadn't been drawing The Far Side for very long, and I was nervous about calling up my editor and complaining. Correcting the caption required sending out a special mailing to the client newspapers (all twelve of them) and I knew it would involve time and added expense. Plus, I didn't want to give the impression that I equated cartooning with a cure for cancer.

On the phone, I explained to my editor what had happened, and he got out his copy of the cartoon and looked at it. After a few seconds, he told me he really didn't think the cartoon had been affected that much by the change. Inside, I died—but I apologized for bothering him and said goodbye. I sat there for a while, looking at the cartoon, and suddenly I realized that, with the caption mistake, it might be interpreted that it's the people *doing the yelling, not the aliens. It was getting worse in my mind. A few minutes later, curing cancer meant* nothing *compared to getting this caption right.*

I called my editor back and tried once again to convince him that the cartoon had been mortally wounded by the caption error. This time he agreed, and cheerfully offered to send out corrected versions to the various newspapers. My relief was overwhelming.

Now, I have to admit that I don't know how interesting this little anecdote is to anyone, but it was definitely a significant event in my cartooning life, because, over the years, lots of mistakes and last-minute changes on both sides of the fence were to take place. And this experience with the "alien" cartoon inspired me to always "negotiate" on various complications whenever they happened.

125

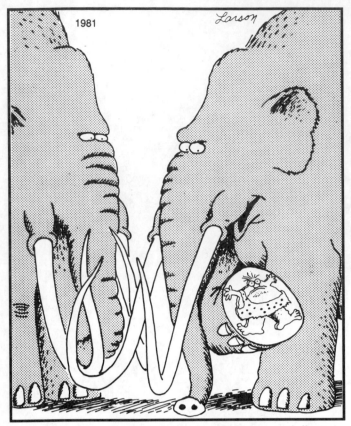

"You know, I thought I heard something squeak."

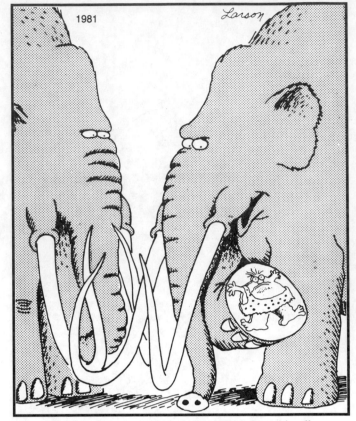

"Well, what the?...I *thought* I smelled something."

I opened the newspaper one day, and The Far Side on the left is what I saw. The version I submitted, however, is on the right. As you can see, there's a subtle difference.

Normally, when a syndicate editor feels compelled to alter a caption, he or she contacts the cartoonist and the changes are discussed. No one contacted me about this one, however, and I cringed when I read the new, wimpy caption. In cases like this, I prefer cartoons be rejected altogether rather than "softened" in their impact.

My editor only did this a few times, and, when the cartoon came up for inclusion in a book, I had the original caption reinstated.

Chronicle Features, 1981

"Lucky thing I learned to make peanut butter
samwiches or we woulda starved to death by now."

Copyright 1981 North American Syndicate.

"Oh, brother! . . . Not hamsters again!"

The Far Side and Dennis the Menace used to be side by side in the Dayton Daily News. *One day, back in August of 1981, someone "accidentally" switched their captions. What's most embarrassing about this is how immensely improved both cartoons turned out to be.*

© Chronicle Features, 1983

"If I get as big as Dad, won't my skin be too
TIGHT?"

Copyright 1983 North American Syndicate.

"I see your little, petrified skull . . . labeled and
resting on a shelf somewhere."

Not long after, it happened again. The Far Side's new caption is just sort of nonsensical, but I think Dennis the Menace turned out rather interesting.

127

"Hey!... You kids!"   "Hey!... You kids! Can't you read?"

The submitted version of this cartoon is seen here on the left. My editor, however, believed something more was needed to clarify why this guy coming out of the house is so mad—so he changed the caption to the version on the right. I acquiesced on this one, but always felt like it was redundant and too leading. I later restored my preferred version for inclusion in a book.

"Well, you've got quite an infestation here, ma'am...I can't promise anything, but I imagine I can knock out some of the bigger nests."

"Eeeny-ooony wanah!...Eeeny-ooony wanah... Eeeny-ooony wanah..."

"Eeeny-ooony wanah!...Eeeny-ooony wanah... Eeeny-ooony wanah..."

A few years ago, the Citizen-Journal *in Columbus, Ohio, made a slight mistake regarding which Far Side caption went with which cartoon.*

The caption for the "slug" cartoon, depicting a mass of slugs worshiping their "god" and chanting some nonsensical intonation, was repeated the following day with the "tree house" cartoon. Instead of the version shown in the upper left corner, what Columbus readers saw was the cartoon at left.

And how many letters did I have forwarded to me asking for an explanation? Don't ask.

"A Louie, Louie…wowoooo…We gotta go now…"

"I'm singing in the rain..."

In a Danish book version of The Far Side, the caption on this cartoon was changed from "Louie, Louie" to "Singing in the Rain."

   My only guess as to why they did this was that "Louie, Louie" was more a national hit than international and the song just didn't register with the Danes.

   And, for all intents and purposes, "Singing in the Rain" is pretty funny.

"That was incredible. No fur, claws, horns, antlers, or nothin'.... Just soft and pink."

The clear intention of this cartoon was to imply that, for large carnivores, eating human beings must be our equivalent of eating Spam—nothing too difficult about it.

A greeting card based on this cartoon was later produced, and the copy written on the inside (by a staff writer) said, "Thinking of you."

Obviously, this addition gave the cartoon a whole new twist—one which I must have unwittingly approved.

My publisher's gift and stationery division decided one day they wanted to make this and a few other *Far Side* cartoons into posters. The problem was this one particular cartoon featured nothing but penguins and ice, which didn't lend itself to color.

When the finished posters showed up, I was interested to see they had indeed found a use for color in this cartoon—they made the one penguin (who's singing "I Gotta Be Me") yellow—the others remained black and white.

In other words, the entire point of the cartoon had been reversed. In the original version, I was being cynical about the futility of trying to be unique in a sea of commonality. But by making just the singing penguin yellow, the publisher made him stand out, and the cartoon then made the same point the song originally intended.

At least that's what I feared. I was really worried someone might actually think I was being sensitive for a moment. That would make me sick.

THE FAR SIDE/GARY LARSON

"Mr. Cummings? This is Frank Dunham in production. ... We've got some problems, Mr. Cummings. Machine No. 5 has jammed, several of the larger spools have gone off track, the generator's blown, and, well, everything seems to be you-know-what."

"Mr. Cummings? This is Frank Dunham in Production.... We've got some problems. Machine No. 5 has jammed, several of the larger spools have gone off track, the generator's blown, and, well, everything seems to be you-know-what."

In my hometown, The Far Side is carried by the Seattle Times, which "crops" the cartoon so that it fits a little better on their comic page.

On the day this cartoon was published, friends started calling me for an explanation as to its meaning. I hadn't seen the cartoon myself (other than when I had drawn and submitted it weeks before) and the conversations sort of went in circles before I got a few clues that something was amiss.

I opened the newspaper to the comic section and discovered that someone, in order to compress the cartoon's size, had chopped off a rather vital part of the humor.

The newspaper ran a correction the following day but, all in all, it's sort of nice for a change when no one understands one of my cartoons but it's not my fault.

SUBTLE THINGS

By trial and error I've learned a few things over the years about some of the more intangible aspects of cartooning that sometimes make or break the final result. The act of drawing is a continuous learning process for me, and I greatly envy a number of cartoonists who have truly mastered their "instrument." I haven't—but I'm working at it.

I assume stand-up comics either work at or intuitively understand things like timing, voice inflection, delivery, body language, etc. (Obviously, they must also have good material, but a lot of good it does them without these other skills.) In cartooning, there are nuances and subtleties in both the drawing and the caption that parallel some of these same elements.

In this next section I've tried to show a few examples of where these things have come to play in The Far Side; sometimes successfully, sometimes not.

"Fair is fair, Larry.... We're out of food, we drew straws —
you lost."

Many times in drawing faces, I find that it's the understatement of an expression that is so very vital to the humor. The dog, in this case, is a good example of trying to accomplish that. I wanted him to look confident and a little smug, but not elated. He didn't get the short straw, but this is nevertheless a serious moment.

"Hey! Look at me, everybody! I'm a cowboy!...Howdy, howdy, howdy!"

I struggled for hours with what I thought was the humor's focal point in this cartoon. I couldn't decide if putting the coat on the vulture was gratuitous or not, worrying that only the hat was necessary. Making a decision between hat and coat versus just hat had me climbing the walls. When all was said and done, I don't think that had anything to do with where the humor was really coming from. In this case, I think it's the tag at the end of the caption ("Howdy, howdy, howdy") that makes it funny. (I should have left off the coat.)

On the left is the first version of this cartoon, which, after completing, I felt contained a fundamental error in showing the action. The second version implies what is about to happen, thereby heightening both the tension and (hopefully) the humor.

"What a find, Williams! The fossilized footprint of a brachiosaurus!. . .And a *Homo habilis* thrown in to boot!"

"Now this end is called the thagomizer... after the late Thag Simmons."

I wasn't sure which section of this book would be a good place to get this off my chest, but I've always felt that I've committed some heresy by doing cartoons (like the ones above) that mixed dinosaurs with primitive people. I think there should be cartoon confessionals where we could go and say things like, "Father, I have sinned—I have drawn dinosaurs and hominids together in the same cartoon."

And then Jake saw something that grabbed his attention.

Thematically similar, I'm afraid both these cartoons ended up generating confusion among some readers. I was trying to contrast a dog's perspective on the world with that of our own.

The first cartoon deals with what I believe is a universal behavior in all dogs: their fascination for one another. When a dog riding in a car sees another dog on the street, there's not much that's going to distract the first animal from checking the second one out. Our own world (which is coming to an end) is not necessarily the dog's.

In the second cartoon, I was just trying to suggest that it doesn't really matter what you do for a living or how big of a jerk you are, your dog still likes to see you come home.

Both drawings imply that, no matter what the circumstances, dogs are, after all, still dogs.

I was nervous about this cartoon when its "debut" approached. At the time, a cartoon depicting a human head in a jar was, shall we say, uncommon on the comic pages. Strangely enough, I never received or heard a single complaint about this cartoon—and I believe the main reason was the drawing itself (of course, The Far Side was only in four newspapers at the time). The point of the humor, I felt, was the innocent fascination children have for things they find almost anywhere—the beach, the woods, etc.—and the fact that this "innocence" was about to come crashing down on top of this pleasant-looking schoolteacher. I was careful, however, to make the head in the jar look sort of silly and benign—any gratuitous details would have distracted from the humor and I think repelled a lot of readers.

"And next, for show and tell, Bobby Henderson says he has something he found on the beach last summer…"

"It's still hungry… and I've been stuffing worms into it all day."

Before I start work on any cartoon, I usually have a fairly good idea what the caption is going to say.

In this instance, and in the last few moments of my deadline, I uncharacteristically made a sweeping change of the entire thing. Originally, the caption read, "Look, but don't touch—or the mother will throw it out."

I still have no idea what came over me that made me suddenly see it another way, but when the cartoon was published it seemed to generate a favorable response from more than a few people. And I always found that to be sort of interesting. Does this mean we all have a latent desire to stuff worms into a baby—or is it just me?

139

Dog threat letters

I think I made an error in judgment regarding this cartoon. The partial view of the dog running away was really unnecessary and even redundant. After all, these are cats, there's a bone lying on the floor, the note speaks for itself (no pun intended), and the title reveals the whole little story. So why did I draw the dog? And now that I look at it again, this should have been a night *scene. I have to move onto something else now because I'm depressed.*

Simultaneously all three went for the ball, and the coconut-like sound of their heads colliding secretly delighted the bird.

When I originally wrote this caption, it read (in part): ". . . the coconut-like sound of their heads hitting secretly delighted the bird." That's the way it was first published.

Then I got a letter from some fellow who suggested, in this case, the word "colliding" would be a better substitute for the word "hitting."

This was quite strange to me. First of all, I had struggled with this caption and never felt comfortable with the final outcome. And secondly, he was right. "Colliding" was a much better word, giving the caption an improved rhythm. So I changed it.

The goal in any cartoon is to create that perfect marriage between the drawing and the caption (if there is one). And this cartoon, I feel, is a good example of when that goal is reached.

Visually, I wanted to capture the look and feel of a scene from an old Bogart film. (I would have preferred the elephant be a little more hidden in the shadows under the staircase, but it's difficult to pull off those subtleties in newsprint.)

But the caption had to accomplish the same dramatic touch. In general, it's risky to write long captions that contain two or more sentences, because it tends to break continuity with the static image. I think this one works, however, because there's no exaggerated action in the drawing. The elephant is speaking under his breath, and Mr. Schneider has turned around and frozen in his tracks. Even if this little scene were animated, we wouldn't see much more movement than what's captured in this cartoon.

"Remember me, Mr. Schneider? Kenya. 1947. If you're going to shoot at an elephant, Mr. Schneider, you better be prepared to finish the job."

Now, here's an idea that just plain and simple didn't work. (Of course, it has plenty of company in that regard.)

I was thinking about Western films and that common scene of some guy getting thrown out the swinging doors and into the street. In this case, every customer in the place is either running or being thrown out—implying that there's a pretty tough and angry character somewhere inside. And how tough a guy is this mystery person? Well, that's his bear parked outside. It's confusing, obtuse, esoteric, and strange—in other words, it's a Far Side cartoon.

141

1985

Punk porcupines

I've never solicited or accepted ideas for cartoons from anyone. For a variety of reasons, I've always preferred to go it alone—sink or swim.

But a couple of days after "punk porcupines" was published, a friend of mine suggested the cartoon should have been titled, "Punkupines." He was right, dammit.

1984

"I've got an idea....How many here have ever seen Alfred Hitchcock's *The Birds*?"

This cartoon has always bothered me because of a basic error: The birds' wings are raised before *the question is even asked. I think it would have been better in this case to have just left the wings down.*

I've always liked this cartoon. And what really made it work (for me, at least) is not just the premise that the deer have to use these outhouses, but also the repeated phrase at the end of the caption. "The deer would come, the deer would come" helps give the reader a sense that Hank is aware that his long, purposeful wait will have inevitable results.

Hank knew this place well. He need only wait….The deer would come, the deer would come.

"OK, one more time and it's off to bed for the both of you…
'Hey, Bob. Think there are any bears in this old cave?'…
'I dunno, Jim. Let's take a look.'"

At the time I drew this cartoon (1984), I don't think human skulls were an everyday sight on the comic page. (Of course, now they're everywhere—I think I saw Marmaduke burying one in the backyard.) With that in mind, I was careful to make sure there was nothing too gruesome about these two characters. Each of them ended up purposefully with an overall goofy expression and just a hint of a smile.

143

1988

"Beats me how they did it…I got the whole thing at a garage sale for five bucks — and that included the stand."

This made a few people upset.

I can't say that that reaction caught me off-guard this time, but I at least attempted to soften its impact with those same people (and my editor) by making the baby's status indefinite. He's not supposed to look dead, stuffed, alive, fake, or anything. It's just your standard baby-in-a-bottle (with stand). I'm just now looking at him here, and, man—that's a big baby!

This never worked the way I wanted.

In drawing these employees taking a work break and playing "marbles" with their merchandise, I realized I could never say the words "glass eye" in the caption. The players already know they're glass eyes and would most likely refer to them in a more casual vernacular—such as kids do with marbles with words like puries, steelies, cat's-eyes, etc.

But I couldn't figure out any slang names for various kinds of glass eyes. (Or at least not before my deadline.) Maybe it would have been better if the caption read, "Just a word of warning, Myron—if you miss, I'm coming after your Albino Water Buffalo #709."

1986

"Just a word of warning, Myron — if you miss, I'm comin' after your big hazel."

144

Another example of when a cartoon's intent was lost on a lot of people. Very simply, I just meant that we all look a little longer and harder at things that fall upon our particular interests.

Circa 1500 A.D.: Horses are introduced to America.

This is one of my personal favorites based mostly on one character's facial expression. The simple "gag" is that Indians and horses are meeting for the first time and handshakes are going all around. But it's the horse gesturing toward the scenery that I felt "made" this cartoon. I can't express it, but there's something captured there that I just like. If I had to draw it over again, the other characters could be drawn a myriad of ways—but I don't think I could ever replicate that one horse's expression.

145

"Blast it, Henry!...I think the dog is following us."

Because The Far Side is a vertical, single-panel cartoon, I've rarely had the luxury of being able to draw long things (like whales, snakes, ships, etc.) in an accommodating shape. In general, the perspective has to be from front to rear, as opposed to side to side. (Sunday cartoons, which I started not long ago, and modified dailies are the only exceptions.)

In cartoon strips, you frequently see the latter aproach—because the strip lends itself well to horizontal images. In The Far Side, as the examples on this page indicate, ships come at you head on, classrooms are viewed from either the front or the back, and riding in the car is often seen from the perspective of the backseat looking forward or from the windshield looking inward. I just can't draw a '59 Cadillac in profile.

I'm saying this because I drew The Far Side for years without truly being cognizant of why I approached it this way. I was just trying to figure out ways to cram things into a little rectangle. It was a friend of mine (also a cartoonist) who pointed out that I had inadvertently developed one or two drawing skills in the process.

The limitation of space I fought in the beginning ended up being the best drawing instructor I ever had.

146

"Yes! That's right! the answer *is* 'Wisconsin'! Another 50 points for God, and...uh-oh, looks like Norman, our current champion, hasn't even scored yet."

In God's kitchen

God as a kid tries to make a chicken in his room.

Drawing God in any context, let alone a cartoon, poses some obvious risks.

In the upper left cartoon, I was careful to do two things: First, I made God look the way I think most of us are pretty sure he looks. Secondly, I made sure he was really winning hands down. Even if Norman had only ten points it would have meant that he beat God to the buzzer at least once, and someone would have gotten mad.

"In God's Kitchen" was fairly benign, since the emphasis was mostly on the earth and the suggestion that things aren't quite normal here and why.

I was mostly worried about the last cartoon shown here. Not because of readers, who for the most part found it to be a light and silly drawing, but because I started to feel like I was bucking for a lightning bolt to come out of the sky and turn me into something like the kid here.

1982

"Hey, buddy.... You wanna buy a hoofed mammal?"

My first caption to this read: "Hey, buddy....You wanna buy an ungulate?" Of course, almost everyone knows that "ungulate" is the collective term for hoofed mammal, but then why risk confusion among a handful of illiterates?

All I just wanted to say about this cartoon was that I think I drew a pretty cool ship in the background. Thank you very much.

1985

"Well, I guess that ain't a bad story — but let me tell you about the time I lost *this!*"

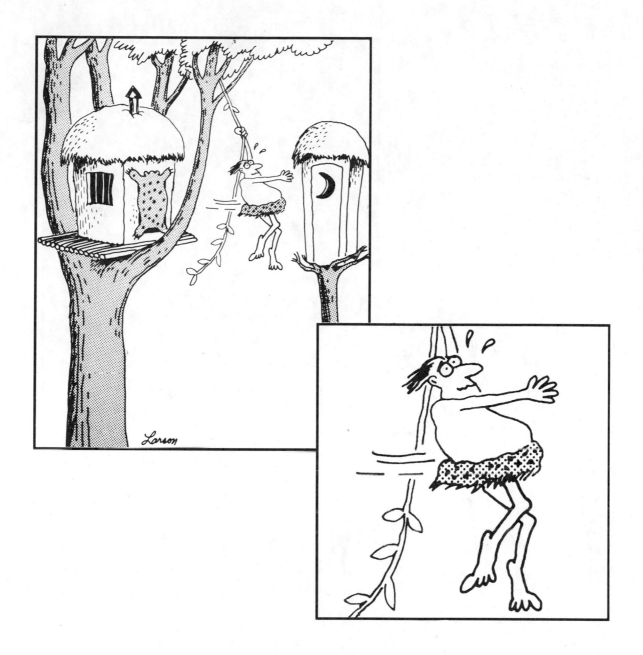

This cartoon was never published. It was submitted in the early eighties when outhouses were still forbidden by my editor. Regardless, I'm afraid the focus of the humor (Tarzan's crossed legs) was a little too subtle in the small format.

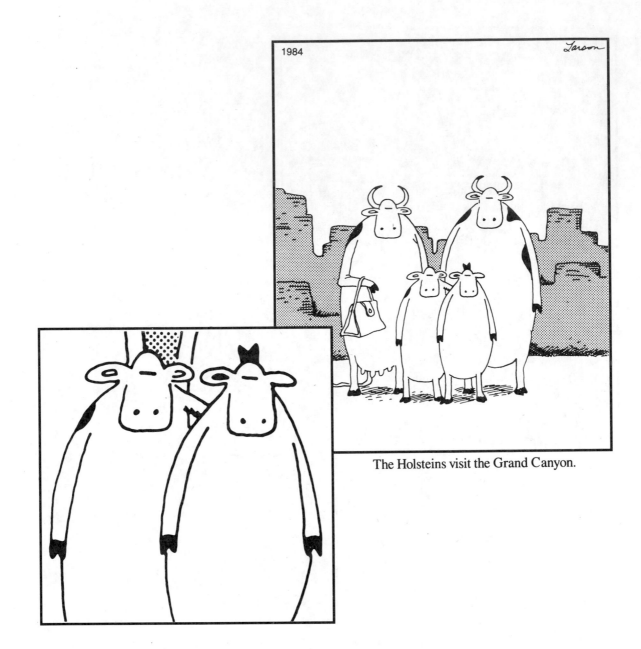

The Holsteins visit the Grand Canyon.

A few days after this cartoon was published, I started getting a considerable amount of reaction from people who enjoyed it. But I found it interesting that, without exception, they were enjoying it from a different standpoint from the one I had intended. If you look at the enlargement of the two little calves, you'll see that one of them is doing the old hoof-behind-the-head trick to its sibling. Apparently, it was just too subtle in the original. (In fact, it sort of looks like the one calf is just wearing a ribbon.) I wish now I had developed this into a series of places the Holsteins had visited. ("The Holsteins visit Three Mile Island" would have been interesting.)

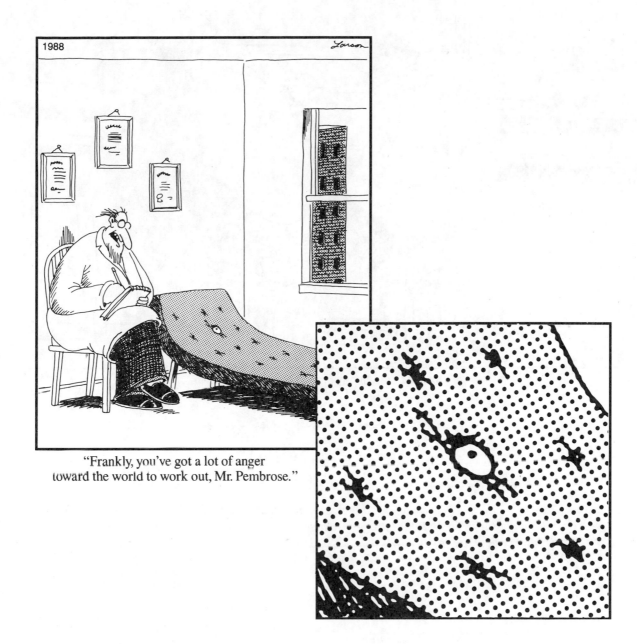

"Frankly, you've got a lot of anger toward the world to work out, Mr. Pembrose."

This cartoon about Mr. Pembrose evidently left a fair number of people wondering what in God's name was going on here.

Mr. Pembrose (I have no idea where this name came from. In general, I just try to match characters with names that "feel right."), from whatever circumstances in his life have rendered him such, is only an eye. (Yes, that's supposed to be an eyeball resting on the couch—the image all but vanished after size reduction.) And who wouldn't have more than a little anger toward the world if ending up as an eye was the card life dealt them?

OK, maybe it doesn't work.

"Just back off, buddy...unless you want a fat lip."

Well, so much for my theory that understatement is an important aspect of humor in The Far Side. Of course, I could make the argument that this guy's nose could've just as easily been made bigger, but my instinct for subtlety knew to play it down.

Part 4
Stimulus-Response

PUBLIC RESPONSE

I have this friend named Ernie. Ernie's sense of humor makes my own seem normal. Every blue moon or so the phone will ring and I'll hear Ernie's voice say, "Hey! I really liked tonight's cartoon!" And then I know I'm in trouble. When Ernie likes one of my cartoons, it means the rest of my readers have just been offended.

In this section I've reprinted some of the more controversial cartoons and the reader reaction each has provoked.

Some of the letters have been published on the editorial pages of various newspapers. Some were addressed to me via my syndicate. In either case, the names have been changed so I don't get my butt sued off.

I've honestly never set out to deliberately offend anyone (well, maybe that one time). All I've really done, like most cartoonists, is just followed my own intuition and sensibilities of what's funny and what isn't. I think there's nothing else a cartoonist, stand-up comic, writer, or whoever *can* do. I mean, it's not that I necessarily wouldn't draw a cartoon like Henry or Snuffy Smith or Blondie, it's that I *can't*. If I drew Blondie, for example, it would still come out looking like The Far Side; Daisy would get rabies and bite Dagwood, who'd go insane and have Mr. Dithers stuffed—whatever that means.

Cartoon humor is strange in that it's a totally silent world of creation and reaction. The cartoonist never hears laughter, groans, curses, fits of rage, or anything. (Actually, maybe that's kind of nice.) It's a daily shoot-in-the-dark approach to humor—some things hit their target and some don't. The target, of course, is anyone who shares a similar sense of humor. The problem, however (and as these letters show), is when innocent bystanders (e.g., Nancy fans) are hit by the same cartoon.

In my own defense, however, I've noticed a frequent common denominator in most of these complaints: They're usually from people who misinterpreted the cartoon. And it's even more curious to me that people often seem angered by a cartoon they don't "get." Well, hell—I don't understand all my cartoons.

In recent years, I decided that the majority of these "hate" letters had to be responded to in a sensitive and professional manner: So I asked my syndicate to do it.

1982 · Larson

Cow tools

The "Cow tools" episode is one that will probably haunt me for the rest of my life. A week after it was published back in 1982, I wanted to crawl into a hole somewhere and die.

Cows, as some Far Side readers know, are a favorite subject of mine. I've always found them to be the quintessentially absurd animal for situations even more absurd. Even the name "cow," to me, is intrinsically funny.

And so one day I started thinking back on an anthropology course I had in college and how we learned that man used to be defined as "the only animal that made and shaped tools." Unfortunately, researchers discovered that certain primates and even some bird species did the same thing—so the definition had to be extended somewhat to avoid awkward situations such as someone hiring a crew of chimpanzees to remodel their kitchen.

Inevitably, I began thinking about cows, and what if they, too, were discovered as toolmakers. What would they make? Primitive tools are always, well, primitive-looking—appearing rather nondescript to the lay person. So, it seemed to me, whatever a *cow* would make would have to be even a couple notches further down the "skill-o-meter."

I imagined, and subsequently drew, a cow standing next to her workbench, proudly displaying her handiwork (hoofiwork?). The "cow tools" were supposed to be just meaningless artifacts—only the cow or a cowthropologist is supposed to know what they're used for.

The first mistake I made was in thinking this was funny. The second was making one of the tools resemble a crude handsaw—which made already confused people decide that their only hope in understanding the cartoon meant deciphering what the *other* tools were as well. Of course, they didn't have a chance in hell.

But, for the first time, "Cow tools" awakened me to the fact that my profession was not just an isolated exercise in the corner of my apartment. The day after its release, my phone began to ring with inquiries from reporters and radio stations from regions in the country where The Far Side was published. Everyone, it seemed, wanted to know what in the world this cartoon *meant!* My syndicate was equally bombarded, and I was ultimately asked to write a press release

156

explaining "Cow tools." Someone sent me the front page of one newspaper which, down in one corner, ran the tease, "Cow Tools: What does it mean? (See pg. B14.)" I was mortified.

In the first year or two of drawing The Far Side, I always believed my career perpetually hung by a thread. And this time I was convinced it had been finally severed. Ironically, when the dust had finally settled and as a result of all the "noise" it made, "Cow tools" became more of a boost to The Far Side than anything else.

So, in summary, I drew a really weird, obtuse cartoon that no one understood and wasn't funny and therefore I went on to even greater success and recognition.

Yeah—I like this country.

"The Far Side, a single-panel cartoon by Gary Larson, obviously went too far to the side some time ago and threw great chunks of the populace into paralytic confusion." —Newspaper Columnist, Chicago

----

"I asked 37 people to explain the 'Cow tools' (cartoon) of last week but with no luck. Could you help?" —Reader, California

----

"Enclosed is a copy of the 'Cow Tools' cartoon. I have passed it around. I have posted it on the wall. Conservatively, some 40-odd professionals with doctoral degrees in disparate disciplines have examined it. No one understands it. Even my 6-year-old cannot figure it out. . . .We are going bonkers. Please help. What is the meaning of 'Cow Tools'? What is the meaning of life?" —Reader, Texas

----

"We give up. Being intelligent, hard-working men, we don't often say this, but your cartoon has proven to be beyond any of our intellectual capabilities. . . . Is there some significance to this cartoon that eludes us, or have we been completely foolish in our attempts to unravel the mystery behind 'Cow Tools'?" —Reader, California

----

"I represent a small band of Fellows from every walk of American Life, who have been drawn together by a need to know, a need to understand and a certain perplexity about what to do with this decade. We are a special interest group under the umbrella organization of The Fellowship of the Unexplained. . . . The Cow Tools Fellows have been brought together by the absolute certainty that your cartoon captioned 'Cow Tools' means something. But, as this letter signifies, just what it might mean has escaped us." —Reader, California

----

"Allow us to introduce ourselves: two humble and dedicated civil servants who begin every working day with a one-hour review of the funnies. Mister Larson, please write us and let us know the message that this comic drawing is intended to portray. As an artist, you have a professional responsibility to your constituents, especially those whose mental health hinges upon the comic relief provided by your work." —Reader, Alabama

Tethercat

The flak over the "Tethercat" cartoon is of a sort I always find interesting. I could understand the problem if these were *kids* batting an animal around a pole, but the natural animosity between dogs and cats has always provided fodder for humor in various forms. In animated children's cartoons, for example, dogs and cats are constantly getting smashed into oblivion by a variety of violent means. (I'd like to know if the creators of "Tom and Jerry" got these letters. Probably, so that doesn't help me.)

What I think I've figured out is, in animation, a cat might be flattened by a steamroller or get blown up by dynamite, but a few seconds later we see him back in business—chasing something or being chased until he's "killed" again. There's never a suggestion that the cat's suffering is anything but transitory. In a single-panel cartoon, however, no resolution is possible. The dogs play "tethercat" forever. You put the cartoon down, come back to it a few hours later, and, yep—those dogs are *still* playing "tethercat." I suppose some people may have appreciated a disclaimer at the bottom of the cartoon saying, "Note: A few minutes later, the cat escaped, returned with a bazooka and blew the dogs away." (Of course, now I'm on the dogs' case.)

"That is sick, sick humor! As a teacher, I know what TV has done to children's behavior and cartoons like this are in bad taste."

—Reader, New Jersey

"With so many sick people in the world today, it doesn't take much to give them ideas." —Reader, California

----

"I was hurt and offended by today's 'Tethercat,' which made a cruel and inhumane 'joke' out of abuse of a small animal." —Reader, New York

----

"Is this the message your company and Mr. Larson want to communicate to the children reading this kind of behavior? It is no wonder at the amount of insensitivity in today's generation." —Reader, New Jersey

----

"Please get on the ball—if you can't print something good and caring, don't print at all. We will be missing nothing." —Reader, New Jersey

----

"If this is Mr. Larson's idea of humor, he could use a good psychiatrist, if this is the idea of humor in Kansas City, thank God I don't live there!"

—Reader, New Jersey

"No doubt some stupid mixed-up weirdo will see the cartoon and get some poor cat and try to emulate the cartoon. . . . I am really offended by this cartoon." —Reader, Texas

----

"We and millions of readers, long-time subscribers, did not like your uncalled-for humor." —Reader, California

----

"More than once I have felt this urge to write my distaste for this particular comic and have wondered over the judgment of the ones who select this type of humor to be sent into the homes of your readers."

—Reader, Florida

"You should be severely reprimanded by animal protection authorities, in newspaper publication and, if possible . . . you should be fined at least $1,000 for each such cruel cartoon." —Reader, Mississippi

----

"As an animal lover I find the suggestion of a cat hung by the neck for the purpose of sport, regardless of the context, to be extremely offensive."

—Reader, Northwest Territory, Canada

"I am seriously thinking of canceling my daily subscription to the local paper because of the sick strips my son read aloud to me about animal cruelty."

—Reader, New Jersey

"Here, Fifi! C'mon!…Faster, Fifi!"

Published in December of 1984, I think this cartoon of Fifi running excitedly toward the braced little door was the first Far Side cartoon to score really big in the negative-reaction department.

In the vast majority of my cartoons where the theme is human vs. animal, it's the animal that usually triumphs—betraying what is probably my basic cynicism toward my own kind (especially my neighbor three doors down) and a fondness for wildlife. When that formula is reversed, however, as in this cartoon, some people find nothing funny beyond what they simply see: a cute little animal about to suffer at the hands of his master. "Animal-lovers" are usually outraged at these sorts of things, often rallying behind the familiar "the-children-will-be-corrupted doctrine."

Well, here's my unresearched, knee-jerk analysis of why it's quite possible for someone to laugh at this or similar cartoons without necessarily being "sick" (or maybe just a little).

First of all, the key element in any attempt at humor is conflict. Our brain is suddenly jolted into trying to accept something that is unacceptable. The punch line of a joke is the part that conflicts with the first part, thereby surprising us and throwing our synapses into some kind of fire drill. (I've read all this somewhere—*Mad* magazine, I think.) And the emotional response to this kind of conflict can range from laughter to a broken nose. In any humorous vehicle (comedy, cartoons, Pintos, etc.), this conflict, whether subtle or blunt, is mandatory.

Back to this cartoon.

Most of the civilized world, I'm convinced, *hates* little rat-sized dogs named "Fifi." The reason has probably as much to do with the type of people who own them as the dogs themselves. But in this cartoon there's an immediate conflict; the reader is asked to accept the unacceptable—that the dog's own master (the standard, heavy-set, matriarchal-type woman) is setting up her *own* dog for an unpleasant experience. Why, of course, no one knows.

So, what you see in this cartoon, I believe, is the classic conflict of one or more elements within a specific context, causing a momentary sense of confusion in the cerebral cortex and ultimately evoking some kind of response. Or, if you don't buy that, then you get to see one of those miserable little dogs getting "bonked."

"Do you really think this cartoon is funny? Obviously you don't think much of an animal to think this one up!" —Reader, South Dakota

----

"The Far Side is funny—if you are insensitive to pathos and so long as the victim is funny looking." —Reader, Connecticut

----

"To me, something is wrong when humor shows someone taking advantage of an animal and that the animal will be hurt." —Reader, Connecticut

----

"Gary Larson's cartoon made me furious. It was cruel, stupid and ridiculous, not to mention hideous, idiotic and sick. In fact, all of Larson's cartoons make me furious." —Reader, Connecticut

----

"This is not entertainment and it is not acceptable to a caring person."
                                        —Reader, Connecticut

"The Far Side is an example of sick humor and does not belong in a family newspaper." —Reader, Connecticut

----

"The comic panel The Far Side should be put on the far side of the moon, where nobody can see it." —Reader, Connecticut

1988

When car chasers dream

Now this one caught me *totally* off guard.

I drew this cartoon in an attempt to capture the ultimate fantasy of any dog inclined to chase cars—that fantasy, of course, would be to actually one day succeed in making a "kill." As a wolf might be envisioned to lift his head above the carcass of a freshly killed moose and howl triumphantly in the moonlight, the "dream" of this dog was to behave similarly over the carcass of a freshly killed Buick.

But I made one mistake. Since the car was supposedly "dead," I put it on its back—never to run again. And since the silhouette of the car's underside was now visible, I drew in the transmission case for a touch of realism. I never should have done that. The place where the transmission would normally go conflicted with where I wanted to place the dog straddling the car—so I just sort of worked them both in as best I could.

The result was another outcry. If you haven't already noticed (and I again emphasize that neither I nor my editors did), the dog and the car appear to be "romantically" entangled. Or, as a friend of mine phrased it, "Hey! That dog's humpin' the car!"

No, he isn't—and I know because I'm the one who drew the damn thing in the first place. I mean, I can reluctantly see how some people might be led to think that that's what's happening. But then, what would the point of the cartoon be? Every dog's fantasy is to make it with a car? I don't get it.

"To some of our readers it appears the dog is copulating with the car. To me it's not as clear, but I think the panel is vague enough to be interpreted that way. I think both the cartoonist and his editors need to consider the possible interpretations when submitting material for newspapers that circulate broadly in the community." —Newspaper Editor, Massachussetts

----

"I think the enclosed cartoon is much too raunchy for a newspaper of general circulation." —Newspaper Editor, New Jersey

----

"This item . . . goes so far beyond the bounds of decency I'm at a loss for words to describe it." —Reader, Illinois

----

"If I've got to start screening The Far Side for obscenity, then I don't need it." —Newspaper Editor, Tennessee

----

"The Far Side . . . has really been in very poor taste. . . .We have three sons in the fourth and fifth grades who read the comics each day, because the paper comes to our house. But today they will not read your paper nor any future edition because we are canceling our subscription immediately."

—Reader, Louisiana

"Please tell me this dog isn't doing to this car what the entire staff . . . believes it is doing to this car." —Newspaper Editor, Pennsylvania

----

"The Far Side is getting too far out. This particular cartoon should have appeared in *Playboy* or some such magazine."

—Newspaper Publisher, North Carolina

"The cartoon . . . exceeded being 'sick' and became offensive. There was no way to avoid seeing it. I do not believe that this cartoon should have been placed in a family newspaper. I believe you owe your readers an apology."

—Reader, North Carolina

"Is this what freedom of the press means to you and your paper? . . . You have that right; however, you have poor taste and lack of respect for your readers also." —Reader, North Carolina

"You know, Russell, you're a great torturer. I mean, you can make a man scream for mercy in nothing flat...but boy, you sure can't make a good cup of coffee."

Every time I do a cartoon about dungeons and torturing, etc., I get a letter from a group called Amnesty International. They feel cartoons on this subject are insensitive to the fact that torturing is something that continues to this day all over the world. And, although I feel my cartoons treat the subject in a mostly harmless way, this group has at least raised my consciousness to this problem.

But what I want to know is, does Wizard of Id get these letters?

I took some heat from a few parents about this cartoon, but this is one that remains one of my personal favorites. It's just such a ludicrous situation trying to pull itself off as a serious one.

I wanted to write back to a couple of these people (I never did) and say, now, c'mon: look at this cartoon: First of all, this cartoon "couple" have not hired a witch-like babysitter to watch their kids—they've hired a witch! Secondly, they're not horrified at what's occurred, as we might suspect, but mostly indignant. And lastly, they're especially upset that the witch ate both their kids—as if to suggest one would have been pretty bad, but both is really unacceptable.

It's even more interesting to me that fairy tales themselves, frequently full of violence and scary things, are directed at children—which is mostly condoned. This cartoon, on the other hand, is merely satirizing a common fairy tale theme (e.g., "Hansel and Gretel") and directing the humor at adults. Now that's confusing.

"Now let me get this straight.... We hired you to babysit the kids, and instead you cooked and ate them *both*?"

Unknown to most historians, William Tell had an older and less fortunate son named Warren.

Reaction to this cartoon baffled me.

Although for the most part I think readers understood the "gag," a few individuals accused me of having fun at the expense of hydrocephalics. Yep—that's what they said.

I hope it's obvious to most people that hydrocephalicus (I still can't believe it) had nothing to do with the cartoon.

Singling out any tragic disease for ridicule would never fall within my own standards—let alone my editors'.

So what do they think about Charlie Brown?

165

1987

"Emma...the dog ain't goin' for the new cat."

More than a few people misunderstood and subsequently complained about this cartoon. Apparently (and I sort of understand this), they interpreted the drawing to mean that the cat had been tied up as "bait" for the dog. That wasn't my intent.

I was trying to create a little story here: This family owns a dog, they recently introduced a new cat to this home, and during the night the dog sent them a message, that the cat's not wanted. The dog did this to the cat. The dog! The dog! The dog!

"I was deeply saddened when The Far Side cartoon depicting a trussed cat hanging by its tail appeared in our local newspaper. I shuddered to think of the children, who, looking at the comic page, might be prompted to carry out this act." —Reader, Ohio

----

"This cartoon today smacks of the idea of using cats/kittens/puppies to train fighting dogs. It is immoral and disgusting." —Reader, California

----

"I was astonished at the enclosed cartoon which depicts a cat subjected to anguish, tied up and suspended." —Reader, New York

----

"I have enjoyed your comic panel The Far Side for years. . . . All this has changed now, thanks to one shockingly awful panel I saw a few weeks ago. . . . The cruelty and sickness of this 'cartoon' was too deep to easily forget —or forgive. . . . A depiction of a person 'hanging' a cat and offering it to a dog is not impossible. I lost two of my cats in similar situations."

—Reader, California

"My letter protested what I saw as a sadistic and pointless Gary Larson cartoon depicting a trussed and hanging cat left to be devoured by a dog."

—Reader, Oregon

1987

"Well, well — another blond hair.... Conducting a little more 'research' with that Jane Goodall tramp?"

A few days after this cartoon was published, my syndicate received a very indignant letter from someone representing the Jane Goodall Institute. Not only did my syndicate and I both get read the Riot Act, there was a vague implication that litigation over this cartoon might be around the corner.

I was horrified. Not so much from a fear of being sued (I just couldn't see how this cartoon could be construed as anything but silly), but because of my deep respect for Jane Goodall and her well-known contributions to primatology. The last thing in the world I would have intentionally done was offend Dr. Goodall in any way.

Before I had a chance to write my apology, another complication arose. The National Geographic Society contacted my syndicate and expressed a desire to reprint the cartoon in a special centennial issue of their magazine. My editor, aware of what had just occurred, declined, explaining why.

Apparently, whoever it was that sent the inquiry from *National Geographic* was shocked. They told my editor that "that doesn't sound like the Jane Goodall we know." They did some checking themselves, and an interesting fact was eventually discovered: Jane Goodall loved the cartoon. Furthermore, she was totally unaware that any of this "stuff" was going on. Some phone calls were made, and the cartoon was not only reprinted in the centennial issue of *National Geographic*, but was also used by her Institute on a T-shirt for fund-raising purposes.

I've since had an opportunity to visit Dr. Goodall at her research facility in Gombe. It's a wonderful place (sort of like right out of *National Geographic*).

"To refer to Dr. Goodall as a tramp is inexcusable—even by a self-described 'loony' as Larson. The cartoon was incredibly offensive and in such poor taste that readers might well question the editorial judgment of running such an atrocity in a newspaper that reputes to be supplying news to persons with a better than average intelligence. The cartoon and its message were absolutely stupid." —Excerpt from the above-mentioned letter that started the ruckus

Bobbing for poodles

"You have offended millions of pet owners with this garbage. If you can not do better than this, we suggest you seek another occupation."

—Reader, Florida

Thank God I didn't go with my first caption, "Bobbing for babies."

And, finally, my response to all those who took the time to register their complaints:

15 March 1989

Dear Mr. Larson:

As you may know, it is common practice for entomologists to name new species of insects after colleagues, relatives, friends, enemies, and people in the public eye. I decided long ago that you of all people should be honored in this manner. With your permission, I would like to name a new species of insect after you. There's a catch, however. I do not work on cute insects. I am a specialist on the order Mallophaga, the "chewing lice". (Human lice are members of another order, the Anopolura, or "sucking lice"). Chewing lice are a group of wingless ectoparasites of birds and mammals that pass their entire life cycle on the host. Even the nits (eggs) are attached to the host with a glandular cement. Because of this close association with the host, members of the Mallophaga are among the most "host-specific" parasites known. For example, one suborder of chewing lice contains 2 species, found only on elephants and warthogs for some bizarre reason. Most avian chewing lice feed only on feathers and skin debris, which they metabolize with the aid of symbiotic bacteria similar to the wood digesting bacteria of termites. In some host families, each species of bird or mammal is host to one or more unique species of lice. In fact, Mallophaga (pronounced "Ma laa fo gaa") are so host-specific that ornithologists sometimes use them as additional characters in the description of new species of birds. "Your" species, *Strigiphilus garylarsoni*, belongs to a genus found only on owls.

If you approve of this somewhat dubious honor, I think I should get your permission before publishing the paper. Like most scientists, I know little regarding the commercial world, and this is certainly not a commercial venture or endorsement of any kind. It is simply meant to honor the enormous contribution that my colleagues and I feel you have made to biology through your cartoons. Can you send me some sort of note of approval?

Best regards,

Dale H. Clayton
Committee on Evolutionary Biology
University of Chicago

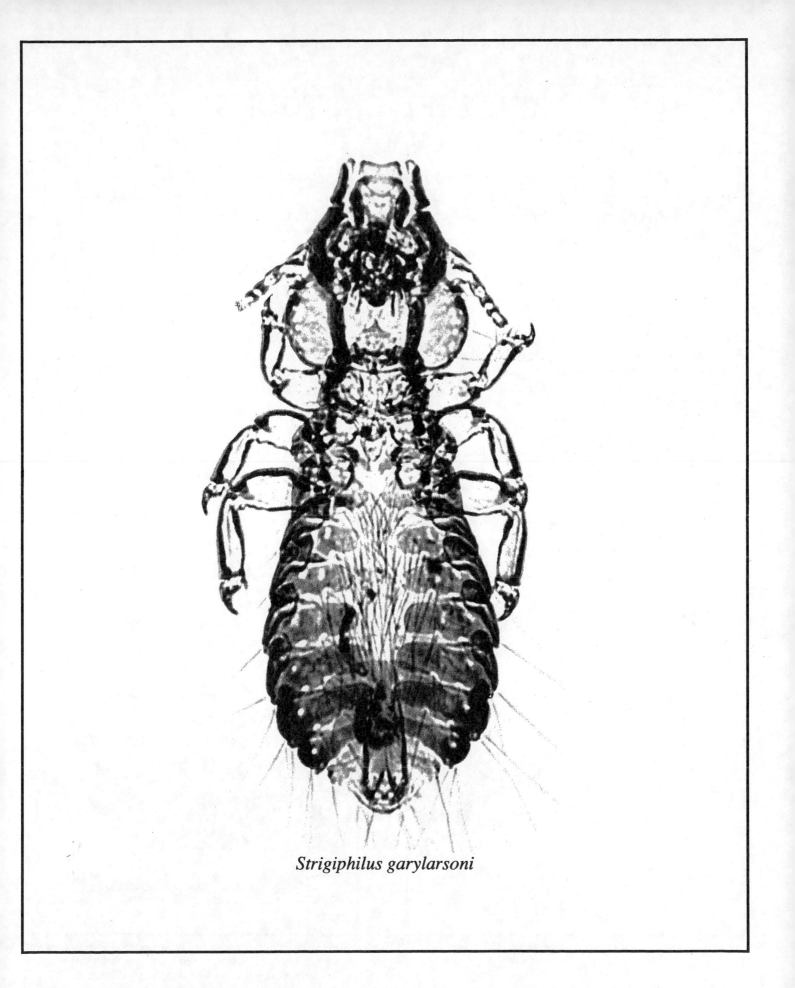

Strigiphilus garylarsoni

REJECTED CARTOONS

The following cartoons were all immediately rejected by my editors. In most cases, their decision to do so probably saved my career. People who think I already push the limits of good taste may want to skip this section.

Figure this one out: When I originally drew and submitted this cartoon, the ants were carrying an older man. That's it, everything else was identical. The cartoon came back to me, unused, with the words "no thanks" written across it from my editor.

I waited a few weeks, and then resubmitted the cartoon—only this time with a baby substituted for the man. And then they accepted it! I'm still scratching my head about that one.

My editor and I both agreed that there were probably just too many horse lovers in the world to pull this off. It never ran.

"You idiots!... We'll never get that thing down the hole!"

"Well, old Roy here said he was hungry enough to eat one, and then I thought, well, shoot, so am I, and one thing sort of led to another... I guess it was some kind of hysteria."

172

I drew this eons ago but never submitted it for publication —for obvious reasons.

"Shhhhh!...the Maestro is decomposing!"

"Well, I guess both Warren and the cat are OK....But thank goodness for the Heimlich maneuver!"

My editor balked at this cartoon initially, not because of the somewhat unsavory suggestion that Warren was choking on the cat, but because he feared not enough people would know what the Heimlich maneuver was.

"I'm sorry, but I ordered sunny-side up -- these are scrambled."

I knew scrambled babies wouldn't fly with most of the civilized world, much less my editor, although I did try to make them look cute.

Just a drawing of a patrol boy and his encounter with an elderly couple from Nebraska. It was rejected.

I've spent the last ten years dying to do a cartoon about dung beetles (hasn't everyone?) but I've always known their very name would present editorial problems—let alone what I'd have them doing. I guess I just drew it for my own amusement.

"Oh, crimony, Warren! It's the dung beetles!... And they've got their you-know-what with them!"

No, you really didn't see this. Turn the page.

Well, what can I say? My editor returned this to me before the ink had dried. If it had been published, I'm sure I would have been up a certain creek without a paddle.

As I've indicated, before the public sees any syndicated cartoons, they're first screened by an editor or two for potential problems. And editors, I'm convinced, have saved my career many times by their decision not *to publish certain cartoons. Of course, that doesn't mean it's any less frustrating when their decisions seem strangely arcane or capricious.*

My editor didn't want to publish this cartoon. I can't recall his exact words on the subject, but basically he felt that not many people would understand the reference to the Wizard of Oz. *Eventually, I was able to convince him to let it go through, and, when all was said and done, I doubt there were really many people who* didn't *understand it. (Strange, when you think of the weird, confusing cartoons they never hesitate to print.) Nevertheless, I can't be critical of these events; my editor's scorecard is still way ahead.*

"Auntie Em, Auntie Em!... There's no place like home!... There's no place like home."

This is much more effective if you imagine sound effects as well. I never even tried to submit this one.

"And now, as I cut the umbilical cord, your baby's life begins!"

" Is it true? Is it true? Is the Pope catholic? Does a bear... Well, I know *you* do, Angelo. "

I thought this was pretty funny, and I think my editor did too—but it was voted down.

I submitted this for publication several years before it actually ran. My editor worried about its impact on some readers, although he personally loved it so much he kept the original on his office wall.

And then one day there was a mix-up over the number of backlogged cartoons, producing a shortage, and this one had to be pulled off the wall and used.

1988

"Hey, Bob...did I scare you or what?"

This was rejected by my editor and never published, but I was never quite sure why. I guess it has a slightly "gross" overtone, but I just meant that ants are fond of egg yolk. Really.

" 'Take me to your leader,' I said... and then the most hideous thing happened."

This very early cartoon of mine was rejected for use in The Far Side. My editor said he would consider it if I removed the drops of "water" falling from the alien's arms. It wouldn't have been a big deal, but I just moved on to other things.

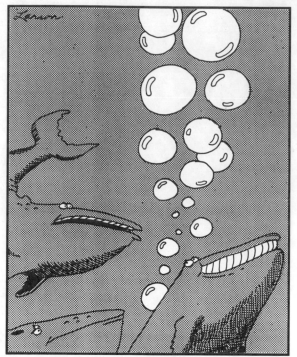

"Kevin!... Was that you?"

"Oh, no! Beans again?.. Well, I guess it shouldn't matter too much in this family."

"Well, it's not me!.. Someone else must be rotting!"

For the most part, any humor considered even remotely scatological is taboo to most editors. In the first years of drawing The Far Side, in fact, I wasn't even allowed to show an outhouse, regardless of how it was handled.

"This is it, Jenkins....Indisputable proof that the Ice Age caught these people completely off guard."

"This is it, Jenkins....Indisputable proof that the Ice Age caught these people completely off guard."

Actually, I rejected the first version of this (on the left) myself. I knew my editor would ponder the good-taste quotient of this cartoon, so I decided not to risk it and closed the door a few more inches.

"OK, here we go again…one…two…"

"Well, just look at you, Jimmy!…Soaking wet, hair mussed up, shoes untied…
and take that horrible thing out of your mouth!"

The Los Angeles Times, *which carries The Far Side, has taken umbrage with my cartoon on several occasions. (Apparently, someone there actually reads the comics beforehand.) These three, as I recall, created some conflicts with the "good taste" standards of that paper, and I believe all three were deleted from their comic page back in the early eighties.*

The first two I suppose are subjective, although I don't remember other papers censoring them. Their rejection of the elephant cartoon, however, had me baffled. I've always found it

"What?... They turned it into a *waste*basket?"

appalling that the demand for ivory has caused these magnificent animals to be continuously poached—but the ultimate act of contempt for the rights of wildlife has got to be represented by the elephant's foot wastebasket. And that's the point I was striving for in this cartoon—not that I was hoping to make a profound comment of any sort (the cartoon is really pretty inane, I think), but just who wouldn't be upset to find out something like this had been done to a former part of their anatomy?

Part 5
The Exhibit

THE EXHIBIT

I drew a cartoon quite a few years ago entitled, "The Real Reason Dinosaurs Became Extinct." The drawing involved a small clique of dinosaurs hanging out together and smoking cigarettes.

That cartoon stayed in my sketchbook for almost a year until, pressed for ideas one week, I dug it out and submitted it for publication. And, lo and behold, it became one of the most popular cartoons I've ever drawn. Obviously, if I'd had any idea of its potential impact, I never would have sat on it for as long as I did.

The following and final section of this book, however, does not include the cartoon just described–nor any cartoon from The Far Side based simply on its known popularity, which would turn this into a sort of "Hit Parade" of weird humor.

Simply put, the following cartoons are among my *own* personal favorites. They're the ones that I feel best reflect something about my own attitude toward history, music, literature, art, religion, and science. (Yeah, sure they do.) I've rarely laughed out loud at the things I've drawn (I'm a little too close to the "joke" to ever be surprised), but these are the cartoons that at least made me smile inwardly. (I might mention that some favorites are in the main body of the book and are not repeated here.)

A final note: I contemplated making this last section a collection of what I consider the *lousiest* cartoons I've ever drawn, but space was limited.

"You meathead! Now watch!... The rabbit goes through the hole, around the tree five or six times..."

"Aha! As I always suspected!... I better not ever catch you drinking right from the bottle *again!*"

"Drive, George, drive! This one's got a coat hanger!"

"It's this new boyfriend, dear.... I'm just afraid one day your father's going to up and blow him away."

1986

189

"OK, sir, would you like inferno or non-inferno? ...
Ha! Just kidding. It's all inferno, of course — I just get
a kick out of saying that."

Professor Gallagher and his controversial technique of
simultaneously confronting the fear of heights,
snakes, and the dark.

1987

Wildlife preserves

" 'This dangerous viper, known for its peculiar habit of tenaciously hanging from one's nose, is vividly colored.'...Oo! Murray! Look!...Here's a picture of it!"

"Well, you can just rebuild the fort later, Harold...Phyllis and Shirley are coming over and I'll need the cushions."

Eventually, Stevie looked up: His mother was nowhere in sight, and this was certainly no longer the toy department.

Another unsubstantiated photograph of the Loch Ness monster (taken by Reuben Hicks, 5/24/84, Chicago).

"Listen out there! We're George and Harriet Miller! We just dropped in on the pigs for coffee! We're coming out!… We don't want trouble!"

The townsfolk all stopped and stared; they didn't know the tall stranger who rode calmly through their midst, but they did know the reign of terror had ended.

In the Fly House of Horrors

"Hold it right there, Doreen!...
Leave if you must! — but the dog *stays*!"

"Details are still sketchy, but we think the name of the bird
sucked into the jet's engines was Harold Meeker."

"My next guest, on the monitor behind me, is an organized crime informant. To protect his identity, we've placed him in a darkened studio — so let's go to him now."

"Listen — just take one of our brochures and see what we're all about....In the meantime, you may wish to ask yourself, 'Am I a happy cow?'"

Animal Waste Management

1988

"Don't listen to him, George. He didn't catch it... the stupid thing swerved to miss him and ran into a tree."

1984

"Ha! Ain't a rattler, Jake. You got one of them maraca players down your bag — and he's probably more scared than you."

1984

Parakeet furniture

The Great Nerd Drive of '76

"Now go to sleep, Kevin — or once again I'll have to knock three times and summon the Floating Head of Death."

"I'm leaving you, Frank, because you're a shiftless, low-down, good-for-nothing imbecile...and, might I finally add, you have the head of a chicken."

Testing whether or not animals "kiss"

"Second floor, please."

"It's the call of the wild."

"Quit complaining and eat it!…Number one, chicken soup is good for the flu — and number two, it's nobody we know."

"And so you just threw everything together?…Mathews, a posse is something you have to *organize*."

202

"Let's see — mosquitos, gnats, flies, ants…. What the?…
Those jerks! We didn't order stink bugs on this thing!"

"Now wait just a minute here….How are we supposed to
know you're the *real* Angel of Death?"

The Lone Ranger, long since retired, makes an unpleasant discovery.

1986

"Stimulus, response! Stimulus, response! Don't you ever *think?*"

1988

"Well, let's see — so far I've got rhythm, I've got music… actually, who could ask for anything more?"

1987

Impolite as they were, the other bears could never help staring at Larry's enormous deer gut.

1983

On Oct. 23, 1927, three days after its invention, the first rubber band is tested.

"You wanna have some fun, Fred? Watch....
Growling and bristling, I'm gonna stand in front of the
closet door and just stare."

"One more thing, young man. You get my daughter home
before sunrise — I don't want you coming back here with a
pile of dried bones."

207

Ship of Fools

Car of Idiots

BOB'S ASSORTED RODENTS

AL'S Small, flightless BIRDS

"Now just hold your horses, everyone.... Let's let it run for a minute or so and see if it gets any colder."

Shoulder Chops

throw-away spare ribs

Farmer Brown froze in his tracks; the cows stared wide-eyed back at him. Somewhere, off in the distance, a dog barked.

1985

How Nature says, "Do not touch."

1986

Primitive spelling bees

1988

"Hold it right there, young lady! Before you go out, you take off some of that makeup and wash off that gallon of pheromones!"

1987

"When I got home, Harold's coat and hat were gone, his worries were on the doorstep, and Gladys Mitchell, my neighbor, says she saw him heading west on the sunny side of the street."

Animal Camouflage

"For crying out loud, I was *hibernating*! ... Don't you guys ever take a pulse?"

"I asked you a question, buddy....
What's the square root of 5,248?"

1986

Only they know the difference.

1987

Dial-a-Cat

1986

"Listen. We may be young, but we're in love and we're getting married — I'll just work until Jerry pupates."

1984

ZOO EXIT

DIRECTOR

"Take another memo, Miss Wilkens…I want to see all reptile personnel in my office first thing tomorrow morning!"

Rusty makes his move.

Laboratory peer pressure

"You know, we're just not reaching that guy."

The conversation had been brisk and pleasant when, suddenly and simultaneously, everyone just got dog tired.

The anthropologist's dream: A beautiful woman in one hand, the fossilized skull of a *Homo habilis* in the other.

215

"Bobby, jiggle Grandpa's rat so it looks alive, please."

"Hey! You!... Yeah, that's right! I'm talkin' to *you!*"

At the rubber man factory

"Oh hey! I just love these things! ... Crunchy on the outside and a chewy center!"

Suddenly, everything froze. Only the buzzing of the tsetse flies could be heard. The crackling grass wasn't Cummings returning to camp after all, but an animal who didn't like to be surprised.

"Think about it, Ed.... the class Insecta contains 26 orders, almost 1,000 families, and over 750,000 described species — but I can't shake the feeling we're all just a bunch of bugs."

1988

1986

"Whoa! *That* was a good one! Try it, Hobbs — just poke his
brain right where my finger is."

1983

"Dang!... Who ate the middle out of the daddy longlegs?"

Dinner time for the young Wright brothers

Piglet practical jokes

"If there're monsters moving in next door, Danny, you just ignore them. The more you believe in them, the more they'll try to get you."

"I don't know what you're insinuating, Jane, but I haven't seen your Harold all day — besides, surely you know I would only devour my *own* husband!"

Aerobics in hell

221

1982

Left to right: Old Man Winter, River, and Higgins

1986

Dang! Tied again!
Ready...one, two, three!

Before paper and scissors

1984

"And now, Randy, by use of song, the male sparrow will stake out his territory...an instinct common in the lower animals."

1984

"Let's move it, folks...nothing to see here...it's all over... move it along, folks...let's go, let's go..."

223

"A few cattle are going to stray off in the morning, and tomorrow night a stampede is planned around midnight. Look, I gotta get back....Remember, when we reach Santa Fe, I ain't slaughtered."

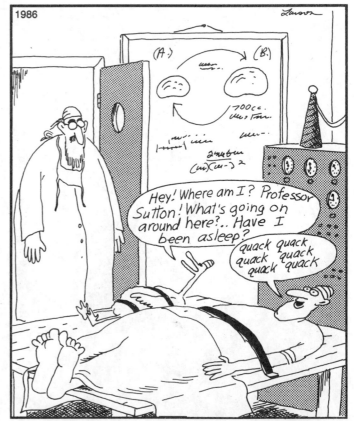

The operation was a success: Later, the duck, with his new human brain, went on to become the leader of a great flock. Irwin, however, was ostracized by his friends and family and eventually just wandered south.

"And that's the hand that fed me."

1983

"I wouldn't do that, mister…
Old Zeek's liable to fire that sucker up."

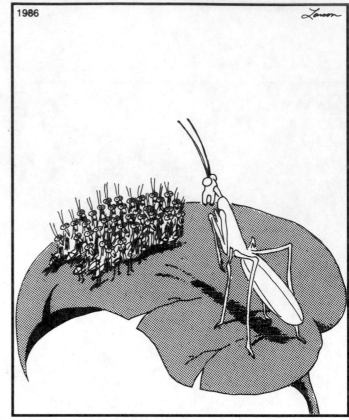

1986

"Of course, long before you mature, most of you will be eaten."

1983

"What did I say, Alex?…Every time we invite the Zombies
over, we all end up just sitting around staring at each other."

1987

"Uh-oh, Danny. Sounds like the monster in the basement has
heard you crying again.…Let's be reaaaal quiet and
hope he goes away."

With their parents away, the young dragons would stay up late lighting their sneezes.

"Egad! It's Professor DeArmond — the epitome of evil amongst butterfly collectors!"

"There goes Williams again...trying to win support for his Little Bang theory."

"Good heavens — just *look* at you! You've been down at the Fergusons' porch light, haven't you?"

When a body meets a body comin' through the rye...

"Relax, Jerry!...He probably didn't know you were an elephant when he told that last joke!"

"I hear 'em!...Gee, there must be a *hundred* of the little guys squirmin' around in there!"

"You know what I'm sayin'?...Me, for example. I couldn't work in some stuffy little office...the outdoors just calls to me."

"And the murderer is...*the butler*! Yes, the butler...who, I'm convinced, first gored the Colonel to death before trampling him to smithereens."

Onward they pushed, through the thick, steamy jungle, separately ruing the witch doctor's parting words: "Before you leave this valley, each of you will be wearing a duck."

1982

Great moments in evolution

1986

"Mr. Osborne, may I be excused? My brain is full."

1984

"Harold! The dog's trying to blow up the house again!
Catch him in the act or he'll never learn."

1987

"For crying out loud, Warren....Can't you just beat
your chest like everyone else?"

"And here we are last summer off the coast of … Helen, is this Hawaii or Florida?"

Cartoon readings

The squid family on vacation

"Do I like it? Do I *like* it? … Dang it, Thelma, you know my feelings on barbed wire."

Suddenly, through forces not yet fully understood, Darren Belsky's apartment became the center of a new black hole.

1987

Ornithology 101 field trips

1982

"Your room is right in here, Maestro."

1984

"You know, Sid, I really like bananas...I mean, I know that's not profound or nothin'....Heck! We *all* do...but for me, I think it goes much more beyond that."

1987

GENERAL STORE

"Somethin's up, Jed....That's Ben Potter's horse, all right, but ain't that Henry Morgan's chicken ridin' him?"

"Well, the Parkers are dead.... You had to encourage them to take thirds, didn't you?"

1985

String (2 ft.)

$$\frac{(your\ age)^2 (mass)}{} = \text{🌍}$$

Creationism explained.

1988

At the popular dog film, *Man Throwing Sticks*

1986

"Now watch this. He'll keep that chicken right there until I say OK.... You wanna say OK, Ernie?"

1983

"Wonderful! Just wonderful!...So much for instilling them with a sense of awe."

1987

Horror films of the Wild

"Don't go in there!"

1981

"Andrew! So that's where you've been! And good heavens!...
There's my old hairbrush, too!"

1904

BOB'S
HONEY,
BERRIES,
& GRUBS

"Just stay in the cab, Vern...
maybe that bear's hurt and maybe he ain't."

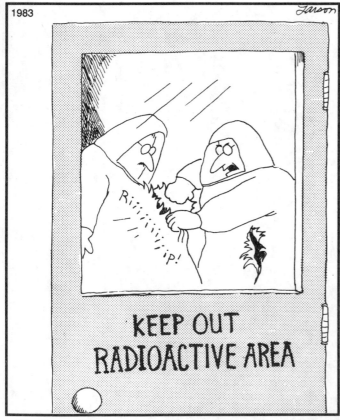

"So, Foster! That's how you want it, huh?... Then take *this*!"

"Oh, Ginger — you look absolutely stunning... and whatever you rolled in sure does stink."

"Notice all the computations, theoretical scribblings, and lab equipment, Norm.... Yes, curiosity killed these cats."

"And see this ring right here, Jimmy?... That's another time when the old fellow miraculously survived some big forest fire."

243

"Now remember, Cory, show us that you can take good care of these little fellows and maybe *next* year we'll get you that puppy."

"Well, I laid four Wednesday, three yesterday, and two more today... of course, George keeps saying we shouldn't count them until they hatch."

The Arnolds feign death until the Wagners, sensing awkwardness, are compelled to leave.

Final page of the Medical Boards

At the Old Spiders' Home

The elephant's nightmare

Same planet, different worlds

"Here's the last entry in Carlson's journal: 'Having won their confidence, tomorrow I shall test the humor of these giant but gentle primates with a simple joy-buzzer handshake.'"

In the early days, living in their squalid apartment, all three shared dreams of success. In the end, however, Bob the Spoon and Ernie the Fork wound up in an old silverware drawer, and only Mac went on to fame and fortune.

247

Nonsinging canaries have to take wood shop.

A lucky night for Goldy

Carl shoves Roger, Roger shoves Carl, and tempers rise.

Killer bees are generally described as starting out
as larvae delinquents.

Cow joyrides

"Well, this shouldn't last too long."

Group photo disasters

"I've got it, too, Omar. . . . a strange feeling like we've just been going in circles."

"Ha ha ha, Biff. Guess what? After we go to the drugstore and the post office, *I'm* going to the vet's to get tutored."

Historical Note: According to some researchers, the final signer of the Declaration of Independence would have been Iggy Fenton if the pen hadn't suddenly gone dry.

Shoot! What a gyp!

Unwittingly, Palmer stepped out of the jungle and into headhunter folklore forever.

"Hey, Norton!... Ain't that your dog attackin' the president?"

Anthro horror films

"Well, I'll be! Eggbeater must have missed that one."

"Honey, the Merrimonts are here.... They'd like to come down and see your ape-man project."

"The boss wants his money, see? Or next time it won't be just your living room we rearrange."

252

School for the Mechanically Declined

As Harriet turned the page, a scream escaped her lips: There was Donald — his strange disappearance no longer a mystery.

"OK, this time Rex and Zeke will be the wolves, Fifi and Muffin will be the coyotes, and ...Listen!... Here comes the deer!"

Buddy's dreams

Amoeba porn flicks

With a reverberating crash, Lulu's adventure on the tractor
had come to an abrupt end.

The committee to decide whether spawning
should be taught in school.

"Bummer of a birthmark, Hal."

"Don't encourage him, Sylvia."

"I'm afraid you've got cows, Mr. Farnsworth."

Through patience and training, Professor Carmichael believed he was one of the few scientists who could freely visit the Wakendas.

"It's Bob, all right... but look at those vacuous eyes, that stupid grin on his face — he's been domesticated, I tell you."

Punk flamingoes

"Whoa! Smells like a French primate house in here."

"Go back to sleep, Chuck. You're just havin' a nightmare — of course, we *are* still in hell."

"Say...now *there's* a little hat!"

Early vegetarians returning from the kill

Knowing how it could change the lives of canines everywhere, the dog scientists struggled diligently to understand the Doorknob Principle.

"Well, that cat's doing it again. Keeping that poor thing alive just to play with it awhile."

At the Vincent van Gogh School of Art

When potato salad goes bad

Where "minute" steaks come from

50,000 B.C.: Gak Eisenberg invents the first and last
silent mammoth whistle.

"Lunch is ready, Lawrence, and... what? You're *still* a fly?"

Poodles of the Serengeti

"I hate this place."

Deer grandmothers

"Well, there it goes again... and we just sit here
without opposable thumbs."

"Listen! The authorities are helpless! If the city's to be saved,
I'm afraid it's up to us! *This is our hour!*"

"I tell you, a crib is just plain worthless — what we need around here is a good cardboard box."

"Say, Will — why don't you pull that thing out and play us a tune?"

"The white whale! The whiiiiiiite wh…No, no…My mistake!
…A black whale! A regular blaaaaaaack whale!"

"Do what you will to me, but I'll never talk!…
Never! And, after me, there'll come others — and others —
and others!…Ha ha ha!"

"Uh-oh."

Butterflies from the wrong side of the meadow

"Kemosabe!... The music's starting! The music's starting!"

"OK, let's see.... That's a curse on you, a curse on you, and a curse on you."

"So, Raymond…Linda tells us you work in the security division of an automobile wreckage site."

1982 Larson

"Oh boy!…It's dog food *again!*"

Early microbiologists

1987

1985

"Watch out for that tree, you idiot!…And *now* you're on the wrong side of the road. Criminy! You're driving like you've been pithed or something."

1983 Larson

"Well, we're lost…and it's probably just a matter of time before someone decides to shoot us."

June 24, 1876: Custer's last group photo

"Yeah, yeah, buddy, I've heard it all before: You've just metamorphosed and you've got 24 hours to find a mate and breed before you die.... Well, get lost!"

"Wendell...I'm not content."

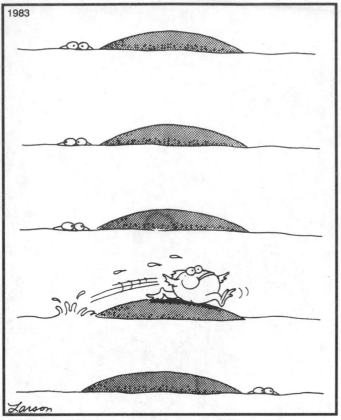

Another great moment in evolution

Nerds in hell

Trying to calm the herd, Jake himself was suddenly awestruck by the image of beauty and unbridled fury on the cliff above — Pink Shadow had returned.

"No, they're not real exciting pets — mostly they just lie around and wait to be fed — although a couple years ago Charles tried teachin' him to take a cookie from his mouth."

273

Jazz at the Wool Club

Animal horoscopes

"Oh, good heavens, no, Gladys — not for me....I ate my young just an hour ago."

"You call that mowin' the lawn?...
Bad dog!...No biscuit!...Bad dog!"

When ornithologists are mutually attracted

Early Man

"Let's see…no orange…no root beer…no Fudgsicles…Well, for crying-out-loud!…Am I out of everything?"

"Sorry to bother you, sir, but there's another salesman out here — you want me to tell him to go to heaven?"

"So! Planning on roaming the neighborhood with some of your buddies today?"

How cow documentaries are made

"Anthropologists! Anthropologists!"

"Why, yes... we do have two children who won't eat their vegetables."

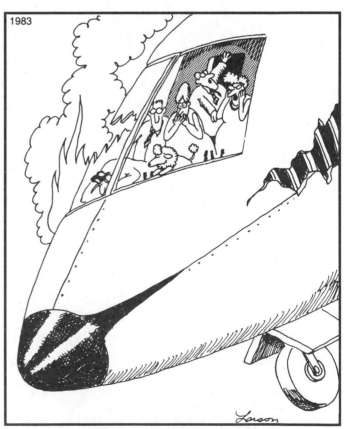

Suddenly, amidst all the confusion, Fifi seized the controls and saved the day.

Dwayne paused. As usual, the forest was full of happy little animals -- but this time something seemed awry.

"Nik! The fireflies across the street —
I think they're mooning us!"

"Excuse me, Harold, while I go slip
into something more comfortable."

1983

"If we pull this off, we'll eat like kings."

1982

"The fool!...He's on the keyboard!"

1985

"Looks like the bank's been hit again. Well, no hurry — we'll take the big horse."

1986

"Hey! That's milk! And you said you were all empty, you stinkin' liar!"

Washington crossing the street

Mr. Ed spills his guts.

Life on a microscope slide

Luposlipaphobia: The fear of being pursued by timber wolves
around a kitchen table while wearing socks
on a newly waxed floor.

"According to the map, this should be the place — but it sure
don't look right to me.... Well, we're supposed to die around
here *somewhere*."

1988

In the quiet of the early dawn, before the village had awakened, Frank and Vern removed the fire god's emerald eye and fled the island -- not calculating how soon the inhabitants would notice their defiled temple.

1988

"Metamorphosis Nightclubs"

"Hey, Johnny! This lady wants to know the difference in all these fertilizers!"

Cornered by the street ducks, Phil wasn't exactly sure what to do — and then he remembered his 12-gauge.

What really happened to Elvis

"Ernie! Look what you're doing — take those shoes off!"

"All right! All right! I confess! I did it! Yes! That's right! The cow! Ha ha ha! And I feel great!"

"Ah, yes, Mr. Frischberg, I thought you'd come...but which of us is the *real* duck, Mr. Frischberg, and not just an illusion?"

Late at night, and without permission, Reuben would often enter the nursery and conduct experiments in static electricity.

"Aha! The murderer's footprints! 'Course, we all leave tracks like this."

"OK, OK, OK... Everyone just calm down and we'll try this thing one more time."